PRAYING
WITH
POWER
WHEN LIFE GETS
TOUGH

PRAYING
WITH
POWER
WHEN LIFE GETS
TOUGH

JACKIE M. JOHNSON

a division of Baker Publishing Group
Grand Rapids, Michigan

© 2012 by Jackie M. Johnson

Published by Revell
a division of Baker Publishing Group
PO Box 6287, Grand Rapids, MI 49516-6287
www.revellbooks.com

Repackaged edition published 2020
ISBN 978-0-8007-3834-1

Previously published in 2012 under the title *Powerful Prayers for Challenging Times*

Printed in the United States of America

To protect the privacy of those who have shared their stories with the author, some details and names have been changed.

Published in association with the literary agency of Alive Communications, Inc., 7680 Goddard St., Suite 200, Colorado Springs, CO 80920, www.alivecommunications.com.

20 21 22 23 24 25 26   7 6 5 4 3 2

This book is dedicated to those who need hope.
May you have the courage and tenacity to believe
that the one who loves you most
will meet your every need—
often in ways unexpected.

May the God of hope fill you with all joy and peace as you trust in him, so that you may overflow with hope by the power of the Holy Spirit.

Romans 15:13

Contents

Acknowledgments

I would like to heartily thank my agent, Joel Kneedler, and the helpful staff at Alive Communications; Vicki Crumpton and the supportive team at Revell/Baker Books; and Hannah Crider for administrative assistance on this book project.

A bouquet of thank-yous to dear friends, family, and my prayer team: Dad, Mom, Monica and Kit Dennis, Jennifer Johnson, Michael and Amy Zenda-Johnson, Maribeth Sacho, Anne Caddell, Laurie Kreuser, Kim Brunner, Barbara Shimek, Tina Wenning, Maria Martellotto, Lynn Carpenter, Tammy and Paul Houge, Nicole and Sumeet Gulati, Cindy and Gary Coy, Erica and Eric Ensign, Diana and Jeff Keener, Judy Gire, Alice Crider, and Judy Downing. I am honored and blessed by your encouragement and prayers.

Many thanks to my faithful Wednesday night Bible study for your prayers and encouragement: Denise Sharp, Doug Platt, Tait Cyrus, Audrey Davis, Sue Eilertsen, Melissa Sturgis, Mary Kimnach, Connie Ekberg, Andrea Archer, and Alicia McCall. To my writer/editor group led by Susan Mathis, AWSA friends, and people with whom I work at Christian Camp and Conference Association (CCCA), I greatly appreciate your prayer support.

I am beyond grateful to those who've been bricks, beams, and mortar in my spiritual journey: my parents, Robert J. Johnson and Patti Ripani, who provided me and my siblings with a spiritual foundation; Lisa Burchell Shimon, who built on that base by pointing me toward a life-changing relationship with Christ; and Pastor Brady Boyd and Pam, who encourage and challenge us often to pray "big, audacious prayers."

Thank you, mostly, to my Wild Hope and yours, Jesus Christ. You are "immeasurably more than all we ask or imagine" (Eph. 3:20).

Introduction

Listen to my cry,
for I am in desperate need.

Psalm 142:6

You see overwhelmed and errand-weary people every day, people who are busy, broke, or barely living. Perhaps you are one of them. Whether you're coping with sudden trauma or dealing with the frustrations of everyday life, you know too well the realities of disappointment, uncertainty, longing, or lack. Maybe you're stressed from trying to balance work and home life. Or you've been unemployed for months and the stack of unpaid bills is piling higher than snow in the Rockies. Could it be that someone you love has left you or passed on, and you haven't a clue how life will ever work again? Maybe you're in desperate need and there never seems to be enough—enough money, enough love, enough time—and you're simply tired of it.

Everyone faces hardship in life. How do you deal with it? When tough times get you down, how do you cope?

Our hurts and heartbreaks form us. They leave an imprint on the landscape of our hearts—some a small dent, others a deep impression. Whether it's a literal flood that destroys your belongings

11

or a flood of tears, the terrain of your heart changes and you are never the same. Outside circumstances or your own poor choices may have left you desert dry or completely eroded, feeling worn and weary. But it doesn't have to stay that way.

The Landscape of Your Life

What is the landscape of your life, and what does it have to do with finding hope? Think of it this way: in nature, a landscape is a section of scenery. It's the view you see on a postcard, on vacation, or right in your own backyard. Picture the rocky coast of Maine, the dreamlike mountains of New Zealand, or the turquoise waters of Bora Bora.

The landscape of your life is a picture of your heart—your inner life. It's a snapshot of how you feel or how you perceive your circumstances today. Perhaps your life landscape feels like:

An unexpected avalanche that has buried your hopes and
   dreams in an instant,
A *war zone*, littered with the unseen land mines of another's
   explosive anger,
A *beautiful garden*, but hidden beneath the hyacinths are
   acres of secret pain, or
Miles of wide-open plains—unexpected spaces in your life
   such as unemployment, recovering from an injury, or the
   stillness of an empty home with the kids grown and gone.

Restoring Your Life

The landscape of your life may be messy and chaotic or perfectly manicured, but how is it functioning? Are you producing fruit or barely surviving? Maybe it's time for a change.

Where I live in Colorado, there's an extraordinary park with gigantic, natural red rocks called Garden of the Gods. Some areas are not open to the public because they need repair, and a sign posted there reads "Area under Reclamation." In other words, "Don't walk here; we're fixing this section." Just as the land needs ecological restoration, the landscape of our hearts needs spiritual restoration—and often emotional and physical changes as well. The good news is that both landscapes and lives can be transformed. Restoration is possible, but often we lose sight of how it happens. We lose sight of hope.

Focused solely on our circumstances, our view becomes myopic; we see only part of the picture. For example, if you looked at a photograph of a desert landscape, all you'd see in the four-by-six-inch photo would be one viewpoint: some sand, a few cacti, and a bit of tumbleweed blowing in the distance. But the picture doesn't tell the whole story. What you can't see beyond the edges of the snapshot is an oasis just ahead, or the desert's end.

There's more to the landscape, and more to your life.

Beyond the snapshot in your mind of how you feel at this moment, beyond your discouragement or desperation, there is more. There is hope ahead.

Wild Hope for Hard Times

You can have hope in hard times—in all times—when you know more fully the one in whom we put our hope. Throughout this book you'll learn more about Jesus Christ, our Wild Hope. He is wild in the sense that he is passionate and powerful, adoring and authoritative, yet often unpredictable. Isaiah 55:8 reminds us, " 'For my thoughts are not your thoughts, neither are your ways my ways,' declares the LORD." While his ways are often surprising, he acts out of ultimate love. Hope that is wild is extravagant; it is beyond our wildest dreams.

Extravagant hope means trusting God to provide the resources when you have only pennies left to your name. It's believing even when you cannot see how things will ever change. When you're desperate or feel as if your world is imploding, it's having the courage to trust that answered prayer is not just for other people—it's for you too. Hope allows you to overcome fear and discover a life you never could have thought possible. Having hope is not crossing your fingers and making a wish; it's folding your hands and saying a prayer. It's *expecting* God to answer, even when you have no idea when the answer will come.

You can have hope for the future and for this very moment because:

- *God is sovereign.* He is in control, and you can trust him even when you do not understand.
- *God is loving.* He accepts you unconditionally, despite your circumstances or poor choices. He's chosen you; he's just waiting for you to choose him back.
- *God is wise.* He knows what he's doing, and his wisdom and ways are far beyond our comprehension.
- *God keeps his promises.* He is trustworthy to do what he says he will do.
- *God is faithful.* He is totally reliable and utterly dependable.

God will provide. He is *with* you and he is *for* you. The good news is that the same power that raised Jesus Christ from the dead is available to you today, and you can access his wonder-working power through prayer.

Powerful Prayer

Restoring the landscape of your life and getting through tough times come through prayer. But powerful prayer is not a set of magic words or superstitious phrases to get God to give you what you want. Of course, God longs to give good gifts, but there is much more. The foundation of prayer is *relationship*. Prayer is a dialogue of talking and listening with the Lord; it is a holy connection with the one who wants to know you and be known by you. More than just *know*, God wants you to *experience* his love, his goodness, his mercy, and his provision.

Indeed, God has the power to make real and lasting changes in your life, but he also desires you to dwell. God invites you to come boldly, to come believing, and to come often to him. A strong spiritual foundation is formed through consistent prayer and, in difficult times, helps you to stand strong.

In this book, you'll discover what powerful prayer is and what it's not. You'll read about misconceptions and obstacles to prayer. And you'll learn the different rhythms of prayer as you behold God in worship, plead for a cause, war for a loved one, confess your waywardness, ask for what you need, and thank him for his provision.

Each chapter includes inspiring words of hope and encouragement along with power-packed prayers (each with its own Bible verse) on a specific topic related to hard times. In essence, you're praying the Word, the most powerful way to pray. Whether you're praying to overcome challenges related to your health, finances, relationships, or other areas, you'll learn more about prayer through biblical examples and stories from my life and the lives of others—both successes and setbacks.

God reveals himself and his power through examples in nature too, so there's a helpful section at the end of each chapter that provides a short nugget of truth, a life lesson from God's creation.

How can you apply biblical principles of prayer to your life? What does it mean to pray "in Jesus's name"? How can your prayers be more powerful? These are just some of the questions that will be answered in this book. Most importantly, you'll connect more closely with God. As you put into practice what you've learned, *head knowledge* turns into *heart experience*—and that makes all the difference.

Instead of lingering in the foothills of faith, you'll climb higher with power-filled prayers on topics such as life after loss, knowing your purpose, unlearning foolishness, banishing worry and doubt, the value of rest, a thirst for God, living connected, God's amazing provision, radical generosity, compassionate giving, and more.

A prayer-filled life is a powerful life. It will help you to stand strong in tough times. When you pray, your life—and the lives of those around you—will be forever changed. You will be inspired to live with greater peace, restored hope, and more freedom. You will discover wild hope through Jesus Christ, a hope so unexpected yet so wonderfully good that when you begin to grasp it your life just may be transformed into one of startling kindness, lavish love, and limitless possibilities.

The economy may fluctuate, your bank balance may rise and fall, and your emotions may ebb and flow like the ocean tide, but one thing is true: "The word of the Lord endures forever" (1 Pet. 1:25). God keeps his promises. He will take care of you. He is totally reliable, willing, and able to meet your needs more than you can ever imagine—wildly more, extravagantly more.

When life is hard, pray on.

Pray On

When the bills are due, when the pain lingers on,
   or the adoption agency is taking too long.
When you're trying to balance family and work,
   or your boss is annoying or simply berserk.
When a prodigal child simply will not come home,
   or the debt collectors won't leave you alone.
When the car wreck leaves you with metal to mend,
   or the man that you loved left you for your best friend.
When you feel overwhelmed—always busy and stressed—
   or you can't seem to focus and your house is a mess.
When you're lonely, depressed, or stuck in your life,
   and you wonder if you're a good person or wife.
When there's trauma or pain, or just day-to-day living,
   or you find that you always do most of the giving.
When you're pondering daily the life you've been dealt,
   with finances, job, relationships, health.
When you're searching for wisdom, or purpose, or faith,
   some heart healing, joy, simplicity, space.
When there's less in your wallet and more on your thighs,
   and your mind reels with questions like What? How? or
      Why?
When you don't understand and you can't see the way,
   you need four simple words: "Lord, teach me to pray."
Don't give up, don't give in, even though strength seems
      gone.
   Just hold on to hope and pray on, friend, pray on.

                                        Jackie M. Johnson

1

When You Feel like Giving Up

Prayers for Perseverance

The Lord is my strength and my shield;
my heart trusts in him, and he helps me.

Psalm 28:7

I
t was just one of those days. The weight of repeated disappointment was so heavy I could barely function. I slumped onto the couch to rest and to ponder it all. Emotional exhaustion can do that to you. So can physical pain.

For months my foot had been so sore I could barely walk. In my opinion, it was taking entirely too long to heal—especially since I was still recovering from another major surgery earlier in the year. Getting around was a challenge, but an extreme lack of funds was getting me down too. It had been months since our company had announced layoffs, and benefits from unemployment were not enough to pay the bills. A note on my front door from the landlord said my rent, already three days late, had to be paid by Friday or

I'd get evicted. There was barely any food in the house because it was too hard to get to the store with foot pain, and somehow it seemed most of my friends were busy or out of town.

Frustration reached its peak when two of my car windows refused to stay up. I'd made my best attempt at taping them, but the strong winds had blown my duct-tape solution away. Cold and rain blew into my car, and I was not happy. It was just one more thing that wasn't working right in my life.

Whose life is this, and what happened to mine?

Do you ever have days like that? Decades like that? If so, I have some good news for you. There is hope.

Maybe you have a different story. Lacrecia is a single mom with four young children. She works full-time and tends to their needs every day. She feels like she's never "off" work. Although she loves her family, some days the endless piles of laundry and messes weigh her down. Drew, a gifted musician, has been trying to get his career off the ground for years but never seems to get a break. And Kara, single for decades, wonders when it will be her turn to have a loving husband.

I hear you saying, "It's too hard. I'm tired. I can't do this anymore." You're tempted to give up. Some days you just want to go back to bed, curl up with a toasty warm blanket, and forget about life for a while. Sure, sometimes we need to rest. In fact, there's an entire chapter devoted to rest in this book. But then what? You still need a renewed sense of purpose, passion, and power to get going and keep going. How do you press on when you just don't have it in you?

Pressing On in God's Strength

Perseverance, according to my Random House dictionary, means to persist, to maintain a purpose in spite of difficulty, obstacles, or discouragement; to continue steadfastly.

If I'm supposed to march on and try to do it all on my own, I simply cannot. Thankfully, I'm not on my own. Neither are you. If you choose to allow God into your pain, he will help you through what Eugene Peterson calls "a long obedience in the same direction." Help is here, and God is with you.

> So do not fear, for I am with you;
>> do not be dismayed, for I am your God.
> I will strengthen you and help you;
>> I will uphold you with my righteous right hand.
> (Isa. 41:10)

Building a Foundation of Truth

To stand strong in challenging times, we need a solid foundation. When we ask, God will build support into our lives so that when the winds of change and challenge blow we won't topple like the fragile houses of the three little pigs. We will stand strong.

Consider what happens when builders construct a skyscraper. In order for the building to be tall and not tumble, the workers first dig a foundation and then pound steel reinforcing rods called pylons deep into the earth. Concrete is then poured into the shaft with the pylons for a super-strong hold.

The same can be true in your life. As you grow *deeper*, you grow *stronger* in your faith. As you immerse yourself in the ways and wisdom of God, the truth (like pylons of hope, trust, courage, and faith) helps you become stronger. So when your life is spiraling downward or you're overcome with loneliness, you will be able to withstand more readily the gale-force winds of hard times and pain.

Steel upon steel, story upon story, a structure is built. Likewise, God's Word tells us that hope comes step by step, as "suffering produces perseverance; perseverance, character; and character, hope" (Rom. 5:3–4).

There is hope ahead. And we're on the way to finding it.

God Loves You

Some people find it difficult to believe that God will actually help them, and the weight of the world on their shoulders is crushing. They think he doesn't care or he's too busy being CEO of the entire universe to be concerned about their unhappy life. Nothing could be further from the truth. God loves you—more than you know. Despite your feelings of insecurity, inadequacy, or any other emotion you're ashamed of, God is all about loving you.

Give yourself permission to believe that what you hope for is actually true. You are not alone; God is with you always. Making life happen, hard and messy as it is, is *not* all up to you; help is available. And it's a prayer away.

When You Feel like Giving Up

How do you press on when you're emotionally or physically drained? When times are tough, here are some vital things to help you persevere with God's strength.

Cast your cares. Don't take on burdens you were never meant to bear—such as worry, fear, and doubt. They'll weigh you down and hinder you from being effective. Instead, give God your fears; surrender trying to do it all on your own to him. Psalm 55:22 says, "Cast your cares on the LORD and he will sustain you; he will never let the righteous be shaken."

Press on in prayer. Prayer is the foundation upon which everything else in your life is built. It is the most important thing you can do. You may think, *I've already prayed. What other solutions are there?* Keep on praying. Talk to God about your situation, because he has the power to change it. Ask God for discernment. Speak freely and openly about how you feel and what you need. Thank him for what he's already done in your life and expect him to answer. As you pray, believe God is working and stand in the strength you receive.

Send in reinforcements. Sometimes you need backup. It's amazing what happens when you receive support in prayer from friends and family members who are willing to pray *for* you and *with* you. When you don't know what to pray, when you're spent emotionally or physically, or, like Moses, when you need someone to "hold up your arms" (to support you), the prayers of others on your behalf can give you a boost to keep going.

Take action. Taking one small step can lead to another and another, and as you build momentum, things begin to change. You will not be in this hard place forever. God will help you through. Unlike others who may have let you down, God keeps his promises. When you take action in prayer, he moves on your behalf.

My friends Cindy and Gary, both in their forties, prayed for years for a child to adopt, and they were on the waiting list just as long. They prayed and waited . . . and waited . . . and waited. Four years passed. Then one day the phone rang with the good news: there was a little boy in Ethiopia who needed a family. Finally! The excited couple recently flew across the Atlantic and picked up their new son.

Holy Tenacity

Is it truly possible to find fortitude despite delays? Yes. Perseverance takes courage. Believe that God is who he says he is: loving, mighty, powerful, and willing to meet your needs when you come to him. When the road is long and life seems impossible, remember that God hears your prayers; he sees your tears. God is with you always, and he is at work in your life.

There are still purposes to be fulfilled—lives to touch, things to accomplish, and character to be formed on the inside. Press on, pray on, with holy tenacity, holding on to hope that one day—maybe soon—the check will come, the job will be yours, or the house will be filled with a child's laughter.

Whatever it is you long for, tell God your heart's desires, and he will answer. Whether the answer is yes, no, or wait, know that the one who loves you most is working all things together for his good purposes (see Rom. 8:28). We may not always understand or like the answer, but we can know with certainty that one day everything will be made right.

Today, we pray and trust him.

A Lesson from Mountain Climbing

A mountain is climbed one step at a time. You begin by putting one foot in front of another, over and over again, until you reach the summit. Mountaineers know the importance of staying hydrated and never climbing alone. As believers, we can stay hydrated with refreshment from God's Word, which is as essential to life as water. We can build a team around us for support and encouragement. And we can learn to trust our guide, Jesus Christ. As you press on, the power of prayer helps you to persevere and find joy. Even when you feel like giving up, believe that the ascent is worth the climb, for once you reach the peak, the view is exhilarating.

FORTIFY ME, LORD

You need to persevere so that when you have done the will of God, you will receive what he has promised.

Hebrews 10:36

Lord, so many times I am tempted to give up. Life is just too hard, and I cannot do it on my own. Please give me the inner strength to keep on going. I long to do your will. Fortify me, Lord. Thank you for keeping your promises—all of them, all the time. I trust you for your help, hope, and healing as we walk through this life together. In Jesus's name. Amen.

GOD'S WORD GIVES ME HOPE

For everything that was written in the past was written to teach us, so that through the endurance taught in the Scriptures and the encouragement they provide we might have hope.

Romans 15:4

Lord, thank you that your words are life-giving power. They light up the darkness in my world and in my heart. Thank you for the Bible, a book that is like no other—alive and relevant for my life today. Help me to read more often what you have to say, to cherish it, and to hold fast to your words. Your words give me hope! In Jesus's name. Amen.

HOPE IN HARD TIMES

We also glory in our sufferings, because we know that suffering produces perseverance; perseverance, character; and character, hope.

Romans 5:3–4

Lord, you know how hard it's been for me lately. You see my tears. Please comfort me and help me through this difficult time. I know you are here, and that makes all the difference. Help me to persevere. Build in me strength and fortify my character. And, Lord, give me hope that one day things will be infinitely better. Like never before I need your help and healing. I trust in your best. In Jesus's name. Amen.

FINDING JOY DESPITE TRIALS

Consider it pure joy, my brothers and sisters, whenever you face trials of many kinds, because you know that the testing of your faith produces perseverance.

James 1:2–3

Lord, it's hard for me to think that something good can come from these challenges. Yet despite my tumultuous circumstances, you lift me up to a place of joy! Joy in my trials? Only you can make it happen. You, who make the sunshine of your love burst forth into my gray, cloudy heart. Thank you. In times of testing, temptation, or total disarray, I need your persevering power. I believe that together we will make it through. In Jesus's name. Amen.

PERSEVERING FOR A PURPOSE

As you know, we count as blessed those who have persevered. You have heard of Job's perseverance and have seen what the Lord finally brought about. The Lord is full of compassion and mercy.

James 5:11

Lord, sometimes it's hard to put one foot in front of the other and keep on going. But you are a God of compassion and mercy. You don't leave me in the desert of desperation. You redeem my life! Job had a really hard life, but he realized that "you can do all things" (Job 42:2), and you blessed the second part of his life even more than the first. When I read his story, I learn that you restored his livelihood, his family (seven sons and three daughters), and his very life. I trust you for your merciful restoration in my life. In Jesus's name. Amen.

2

When You're Busy and Stressed

Prayers for Peace and Rest

> I will refresh the weary and satisfy the faint.
>
> Jeremiah 31:25

It was late when I finally finished eating dinner. Tired and bleary-eyed from a long week at work, I opened the kitchen cupboard to put away my spaghetti leftovers and stopped suddenly. *What am I doing?* I shook my head and laughed and put the food in the refrigerator where it belonged. I was exhausted. The past few months had been a whirlwind, and tension was taking its toll. Of course, putting Italian food in the wrong place was the least of it. Most nights I was up late working, folding laundry, or doing "one more thing" before going to bed, wondering why the days were so long and the nights so short.

I don't think I'm the only one who has too much to do and never enough time. Recently, Amanda's company had layoffs. While she's glad to still have a job, she's overloaded with work now that her firm employs significantly fewer people. Rachel is a stay-at-home mom with three kids under age four who laughs when you say the word *rest*, since she never seems to get enough. And Darnell, who works three jobs just to get by, wonders when he will ever get a good night's sleep.

Indeed, we are a generation of busy people—working hard but hardly living. Getting enough rest, replenishing rest, is often at the bottom of our priority lists. But why?

So Many Reasons, So Little Time

We all have our reasons why we don't make rest a priority. Some are self-imposed. Some people stay continually busy in order to avoid pain and disappointment. Others live a life of constant activity because they're trying to please others or keep up appearances. I've heard bleary-eyed nine-year-olds complain about their packed weekly routine of soccer, piano, and dance, in addition to school and homework, because it's what their parents want.

Of course, people have busy seasons in life, like a couple with a newborn baby or an accountant during tax time. But for some, being busy all the time seems to be a badge of honor. Have you ever run into someone you haven't seen in a while and said, "Hi! How are you?" and she replies, "Good. I'm *so busy* these days"?

In the exhaustion of daily living, we often complain, "There's so much to do and never enough time," instead of saying a quiet prayer, "Lord, I am so tired. Please help me." And that's exactly what God will do when you ask him. There is a better way to find a better life, but sometimes false beliefs keep us stuck on a hamster wheel of perpetual motion.

Lies We Believe about Rest

To be sure, there is a time to work. God uniquely created each of us with talents and abilities to make a contribution in life. We may be good at what we do and find satisfaction in a job well done. But there is also a time to cease from our labor.

Being driven is one thing; being a slave to what we do—bound by guilt, condemnation, perfectionism, or people-pleasing—is bondage. Unknowingly, we are living a lie.

"The lie the taskmasters want you to swallow is that you cannot rest until your work's all done, and done better than you're currently doing it," said Mark Buchanan in *The Rest of God*. "But the truth is, the work's never done, and never done quite right. It's always more than you can finish and less than you had hoped for."[1]

If we address some of the lies and release them, then physical rest and inner peace—soul rest—can replace worry and fear, and things can begin to change. Read each lie listed here and talk to God about what is keeping you from getting the rest you need.

- *Lie: I can do everything and do it all on my own.* A person who believes this lie thinks she has to make everything happen, do everything for everyone, and do it all by herself. Some may call her a martyr; others may call her a control freak. She believes her way is the "right" way and that she must save the world. The truth is that we are sorely deceived when we think we are a junior Jesus. We don't save the world; he already did that for us. It's the ultimate deception when we think we are like God or we are God (see Gen. 3:5).

- *Lie: Rest is a luxury for a privileged few.* I used to think this when I was short on funds and working three jobs just to stay afloat. It didn't seem fair, but I felt guilty when I rested. Then I came across the book *When I Relax I Feel*

Guilty by Tim Hansel and learned that I had a right to rest. In fact, rest was God's idea (see Gen. 2:2–3).

- *Lie: I don't deserve to rest.* Rest is a gift. You don't earn it. A slave-driver mentality is not from God but from the enemy, the one who is out to destroy you. The truth is that when you come to know Christ you are set free (see John 8:36).

- *Lie: Rest is a waste of time.* In reality, taking time to renew your weary self is time well spent. It's an investment that will pay off physically, mentally, emotionally, and relationally because you will be a better you—for others and for yourself. Stopping periodically to get refreshed ultimately helps you get the job done more effectively.

- *Lie: If I rest, I won't get it all done.* This lie goes back to the fundamental question of whose agenda we are following. A major heart shift happens when we begin to realize that life is about God's plan, his story. We live for God, not for ourselves. He will enable us to get done what he wants accomplished each day when we are surrendered and willing.

The Value of Rest

I am a lot like my German grandmother, Lena. She constantly bustled around the kitchen making spaetzle and sauerkraut, and it took some doing to get her to actually sit down at the dinner table with the rest of us. Like her, I want to get stuff done. I have many lists and find satisfaction in crossing off what I've accomplished. While it's true that being productive can be a good thing, I've often gone to extremes, and it has taken me time to learn the value of rest. Rest is essential for many reasons.

Rest is necessary, both physically and emotionally. It's essential to life and good health. Sometimes we are so preoccupied with trying to *gain* more in life that we often fail to realize what is *lost* in the process. In the demanding pace of life, we may lose perspective, forget things, or mess up our priorities. We lose peace of mind and connection with God and others. Our health and relationships suffer. We feel cranky, scattered, or alone. In our efforts to be *efficient*, we may not always be *effective*. Often, we lose heart.

And we need to find it again.

Perhaps we don't value rest because we've forgotten what it means. Our perception may be skewed by a culture that praises busyness and devalues silence, stillness, and reflection.

Rest brings margin to your life, spaces that allow you to replenish and restore beauty and balance. Without it, life is an endless cycle of work, chores, and errands. And that's not what God intended. Joy, peace, fun, and play are essential parts of life too.

Consider a score of music. Without well-placed rests, beats of silence, a song would run on and on; it would fail to achieve its true purpose. And it would surely weary the listener's ear. So composers use whole, half, or quarter rests—longer or shorter beats—to make beautiful music. Is there a way for you to find some well-placed rests in your own life? For example:

A quarter rest, which is brief, could be a ten-minute walk to clear your head and say a short prayer. Often, I get my best ideas when I get up from my desk and have a change of scenery.

A half rest could be a weekend away or even getting a restful night's sleep.

A whole rest, a longer period of time, could be a much-needed vacation or spiritual retreat.

Replenishing rest looks different for everyone. Whether it's lingering over a cup of tea with a friend, taking a nap, or enjoying a one-minute vacation gazing at the Hawaiian beaches on your wall calendar, think about how you can get refueled in your life, because when we're well-rested, we are better equipped to serve God and others—and enjoy our lives.

Rest is trusting God. Busyness is the amount of activity in your life; stress is how you handle it—or don't. You were never meant to do life on your own or carry the weight of the world like boulders in a backpack. When you release your worries to God, you're saying that you trust him. Instead of being anxious, you can rely on the fact that God said he would take care of all your needs. God is always at work, even when you're asleep. When you are feeling overwhelmed, say to yourself, "I cannot, but God can." God can do anything; nothing is too hard for him, even restoring peace to your whirlwind life.

Rest is God's idea. God gives you permission to rest. In fact, it was his idea from the beginning. In the first book of the Bible, Genesis, we learn that God created the heavens and the earth "in all their vast array" (Gen. 2:1). Imagine the sheer delight of God, the master artist and architect, forming star-studded galaxies, planets that spin, and gravity to tether us all to the earth. After he created, he rested (whatever that looks like for God) and gave us a pattern to follow for our own lives.

> The heavens and the earth were completed in all their vast array. By the seventh day God had finished the work he had been doing; so on the seventh day *he rested from all his work.* Then God blessed the seventh day and made it holy, because on it he rested from all the work of creating that he had done. (Gen. 2:1–3, emphasis added)

Jesus knew well the importance of rest. He had three years, only a short time, to accomplish his mission, yet he often left the crowds to get away and pray. He invites us to lay down our burdens and find real rest in the "unforced rhythms of grace," as the Message explains:

> Come to me. Get away with me and you'll recover your life. I'll show you how to take a real rest. Walk with me and work with

me—watch how I do it. Learn the unforced rhythms of grace. I won't lay anything heavy or ill-fitting on you. Keep company with me and you'll learn to live freely and lightly. (Matt. 11:28–30)

Jesus knew that in order to be about his Father's business, he needed to be connected in prayer to God the Father. How can we be empowered to live our full lives? By releasing our cares and making prayer a priority.

Making Prayer a Priority

Life is a marathon, not a sprint. We need to pace ourselves. Instead of constantly getting caught up in the *urgent* things in life, we can find a way to attend to the *important* things when we remember to pray. Take a look at your schedule. Have you built in any time for prayer, for rest, for fun? As you reprioritize, ask yourself what you can delegate or let go of (either for now or forever). Then make a decision to put prayer on your to-do list each day. It will not only build your relationship with God (the primary purpose) but also give you the power and strength to accomplish what he wants done for that day—and beyond.

Maya made a courageous choice recently. A director at a telecommunications company, she had been working eighty hours a week or more for nearly twenty years. The stress was literally killing her. She learned that her blood pressure was skyrocketing into dangerously high zones, and the late-night work sessions and pre-dawn meetings were taking their toll on her relationships—and her life. She didn't take time to connect with God, exercise, or eat well. Something had to change.

So she took an emergency week off work to rest (sleeping sixteen hours per day) and began taking hypertension medicine. She talked with her boss and set some limits, like no phone calls before 7:00 a.m. But the fast pace continued, and her health got worse.

So her doctor prescribed short-term disability so she could get her health under control. Maya spent weeks crying and crying out to God, wondering what to do. If her life had to change drastically, it would mean a huge shift in her identity. She wondered, *Who will I be if I'm not a corporate executive?* Maya had a hard time believing she was loved by God just for being her—not what she did for a living.

In the ensuing weeks, Maya kept praying—and she began to change. God was clearly showing her that it was time to move on from this demanding pace. Once she decided to obey God, her health improved and her energy returned. It has taken time for Maya to accept a slower but healthier way of living, but she's glad to be connecting more with God and the people she cares about most. She trusts God with each day, and she is encouraged and excited.

When you choose to make prayer a priority, you are really choosing God. That's because prayer is a one-on-one conversation with your Creator. He knows you better than anyone, even better than you know yourself! Build your relationship with God as you would with a close friend. Talk, listen, and find out more about his character. You'll gain insight, wisdom, and strength to face life's challenges.

You may not always have a large block of time to pray. Some women I know pray as they're feeding their baby or driving to work. But make every effort to be alone with God in a quiet place, to spend time with the one who loves you most. That's where you will find the power to live and the peace you crave.

Choose to make prayer a priority every day. Talk with God, trust in him, rest on the inside even as you work. You may even look up, smile, and say a simple "Thank you."

Your days may be full, but your heart doesn't have to be empty or anxious. Powerful prayer begins as you release your cares, connect with God, and allow him to work through you. Then enjoy the love and peace, freedom and power that are yours.

Yes, my soul, find rest in God;
my hope comes from him. (Ps. 62:5)

A Lesson from God's Creation

God created the natural world, and the beauty of his creation renews us. We are replenished when we see pine trees covered with fresh, white snow on a winter's day. Even when you can't get outdoors, imagine the gentle sound of ocean waves as they lap against the shore, washing away your cares. Picture yourself walking in a quiet place: along a sandy beach, in a sunlit forest, or atop a magnificent mountain peak. God created all this for you to enjoy, and more than that, he is with you. Always. Be at peace.

FEELING OVERWHELMED

Now may the Lord of peace himself give you peace at all times and in every way.

2 Thessalonians 3:16

Lord, I am frazzled. My hands are full and my mind is reeling with all the things I have to do. Please help me to accomplish all that needs to get done each day and to find rest. As I work, help me to be productive and peaceful. As I love others, help me to be calm and encouraging. I need your peace in every area of my life today. In Jesus's name. Amen.

A QUIET PLACE

Come with me by yourselves to a quiet place and get some rest.

Mark 6:31

Lord, I need you. I need your peace and rest. You are calling me to come, and yet I hesitate. I want to relax, but often I feel guilty. What will happen if I lay down my worries and cares? People are depending on me. I'm afraid life will fall apart. But when you call, I will come. I will choose to be with you to replenish. Help me to recharge so I can be a better me for others, for myself, and mostly for you. I choose you first. You, Lord, are my peace. In Jesus's name. Amen.

REST IS TRUSTING GOD

On him we have set our hope that he will continue to deliver us.

2 Corinthians 1:10

Lord, I'm so tired. You know how things have been for me lately. I know that I cannot put my primary hope in anything but you. Not money, or people, or things. Help me to remember that I can have peace because you have a plan. I can rest because I can trust you. You promised to provide, and you will. You promised to take care of me, and you will. Give me courage to rely on you completely. My hope is set on you. In Jesus's name. Amen.

GOD IS WITH ME ALWAYS

The Lord replied, "My Presence will go with you, and I will give you rest."

Exodus 33:14

Lord, I cannot tell you what it means to me that your presence is with me. In hard times, in all times, it comforts me to know you are near. Here. With me. Thank you for your love and provision. My days may be full, but I always want to put you first and lean on you for all that I need. You promised rest, and I will receive your gift. Help me to find strength in the stillness and then go about my day knowing you are always near. In Jesus's name. Amen.

STRENGTHEN ME, LORD

I can do all this through him who gives me strength.

Philippians 4:13

Lord, it feels like there's so much to accomplish each day, and sometimes it's hard to rest. I'm afraid I won't get it all done. I'm afraid I will fail. Yet you promise to strengthen me. You are the mighty God! Help me to focus on what you can do, not what I cannot. Empower and encourage me. Give me the lasting strength only you can give. Replenish me so I can live life better and stronger. In Jesus's name. Amen.

GETTING MY PRIORITIES IN ORDER

But seek first his kingdom and his righteousness, and all these things will be given to you as well.

Matthew 6:33

Lord, I have my agenda, but what do you want done today? Help me to prioritize all that needs to get done. In the midst of life's busyness, help me to be centered on what's truly important and not always get caught up in the urgent. Help me to put you first, for I know that from my replenishing time with you all else flows. I will seek you first. In Jesus's name. Amen.

FINDING HOPE, JOY, AND PEACE

May the God of hope fill you with all joy and peace as you trust in him, so that you may overflow with hope by the power of the Holy Spirit.

Romans 15:13

Lord, in the middle of my stressed-out life, I'm glad that you are my hope! As I strive to balance work, family, and life commitments, I need to remember to ask for help from the one who can do all things. Forgive me for trying to do it all on my own. Renew my energy and my joy. Invigorate me for all you have for me in this season of life. May I find inner calm despite outer circumstances. In Jesus's name. Amen.

REST FOR THE WEARY

Come to me, all you who are weary and burdened, and I will give you rest. Take my yoke upon you and learn from me, for

I am gentle and humble in heart, and you will find rest for your souls. For my yoke is easy and my burden is light.

Matthew 11:28–30

Lord, I am so grateful for rest. It was your idea in the first place! Instead of tossing and turning at night with eyes wide open, I give you my worries and cares, my lists and schedules. With open hands, help me to release all I cling to so tightly. I need rest for my spirit and my body. Let me live from a calm and grounded center as I come to you each day. In Jesus's name. Amen.

3

When Life Is a Mess

Prayers for Simplicity and Order

Jesus replied, "What is impossible with man is possible with God."

Luke 18:27

My friend Christi has been doing some extreme cleaning lately. Both of her parents have passed away, her father most recently, and she's been charged with cleaning out the home they lived in for decades. The challenge is that both of them were hoarders; they simply could not throw anything away. Surrounded by massive clutter—with ceiling-high piles, papers, and multiples of items saved over a forty-year span—Christi feels overwhelmed. *How will I ever get this mess cleaned up?* she wonders.

There are all kinds of messes in life: physical, emotional, spiritual, and financial. And there are different levels of messiness too, from untidiness to totally chaotic to somewhere in between.

I didn't know much about getting organized until well into my twenties. When one of my roommates asked me why I stuffed all my papers and bills into a small nightstand, I was at a loss. I didn't have a clue what to do with them, so I just kept stuffing until the nightstand was overflowing. Thankfully, Marion was kind enough to tell me about file folders and how to use them. She gathered a pile of manila folders and a marker and told me to label each one, insert the corresponding papers, and put them in alphabetical order.

It all seemed so easy for her, but as a young woman, it was as foreign to me as boarding a train in Borneo and not knowing the language. Her organizing help changed my life. Once I removed the physical clutter in my room, I felt lighter inside and more at peace. It was liberating.

Like stuffing papers in a nightstand, sometimes we stuff our emotional junk and create a heart mess. We hold in massive amounts of pain or rage until one day the emotions leak out, often at inappropriate times. Or we're just not good at managing our finances, and we end up in financial disaster. Creditor calls become the norm, and bankruptcy looms just around the corner.

Life can be messy and often complicated. I get it. Your life may be more disorder than disaster. Each day is a rerun of wiping up after kids with muddy shoes. Or you have piles of papers on your dining room table and scurry to hide them when company comes. Or you're running from meeting to meeting, airport to airport, and never seem to have time to organize a "real life." Or could it be that your home is spotless, like a veritable showroom with things perfectly in place, but the one thing that matters most is not?

Your heart.

What does your heart look like? Is it littered with garbage from the past, like hurts you just can't seem to release, or the waxy buildup from daily stresses? Maybe it's time to clear away some anger or finally forgive someone. Your heart needs to be cleansed, healed, and filled on a daily basis. And you can do that every day—every moment—when you come to God in prayer.

Obstacles to Ordered Hearts

You may have good intentions. You want to be right with God. You desire to pray, or pray more often, and have an ordered heart, one that's clean and pure. Peace sounds really good, and you could use a large dose of contentment. But there are obstacles. I can hear the excuses now; I've said them myself. *I'm too tired. I don't have any energy. I don't have time; my life is too full right now. I don't want to deal with those things. I don't know how. I just don't care.* We have many excuses to avoid dealing with emotional pain or confronting spiritual disarray.

It's time for a new perspective.

"Jesus can redeem our past," says Michael Yaconelli, "no matter what kind of past we bring with us: failure, mistakes, bad decisions, immaturity, and even a past which was done to us."[1]

When I was younger, I often wished there was a book on how to fix broken lives and clean up messes, one that would help me know what to do to make things right again. And then I found it. It's called the Bible. From beginning to end (from Genesis to Revelation), the Bible is chock-full of stories of God restoring the messed-up lives of men and women—even seemingly "good people."

Here are two examples. Sarah wanted a baby and took matters into her own hands. She had her husband sleep with her maidservant, then got jealous and made a mess of things for years to come. The descendents of the child born to the maidservant, Ishmael, and the child Sarah eventually bore, Isaac, are still clashing in the Middle East today. Or consider David. He was a king who loved God, yet he committed adultery with Bathsheba and killed her husband in an attempt to cover it up.

What a mess.

God is all about fixing broken things and restoring hearts, for people long ago and for us today. You can clear the clutter and change your life as you talk with God in prayer. And unlike spring cleaning, which happens only once a year, you can come at any time. God is always there.

Relationship First

The one who loves you most wants to help you with your stuff, but first he wants a relationship with you—a healthy, ongoing, connected love relationship. You want to know and be known, to love and be loved. So does he. We connect with God because we love him, and connection is also where the power to change comes from. Jesus said, "I am the vine; you are the branches. If you remain in me and I in you, you will bear much fruit; apart from me you can do nothing" (John 15:5). Apart from God we cannot; with God we can! His life-giving power courses through our lives, like sap nourishes a tree or a vine. That's where the life is; that's where the growth comes from.

Restoring Order

God is willing and more than able to restore your life. The results may not always look like you think they should and may not happen in this lifetime. But as you trust in him, by faith, he will make all things new and bring order to every area of your life. God can help you to:

Order your heart to make room for God and connect with him on deeper levels

Order your emotions and clear out lingering anger, bitterness, and pride to increase your joy and contentment

Order your thoughts and get rid of mental clutter so you can focus on your priorities—like getting in shape or spending your time and money more effectively

Order your home so you can find the things you need and have more freedom and peace

Prayer Changes Things

Prayer is vital to making significant life changes. As you come to God in prayer, ask him to cleanse, heal, and restore every area of your life.

Cleanse

We get hurt, or we hurt others, so our hearts need to be cleansed of sin and wrongdoing often. Ask God, "What do I need to release?" Maybe you need to let go of resentment, offense, bitterness, or a judgmental attitude. Whatever it is, ask God for forgiveness and cleansing in your life. When we are repentant, God forgives us, and it feels like clear water washing away the dirt.

Heal

Ask God to reveal to you what needs to be healed in your heart or in your life. You may already know, but you may not. Then ask God to heal you. It may come suddenly or over time; God works differently at different times, but he is always at work.

Restore

After you are cleansed and healed, ask God to fill you. Receive your restoration. Ask God, "What do I need to add to my life?" You've *taken off* or released things that have hindered you; now *put on* or "clothe yourselves with compassion, kindness, humility, gentleness and patience" (Col. 3:12).

Restoration Is a Process

As God brings order to your life, remember that it's a process. Going from mess to order or from chaos to simplicity doesn't happen overnight. Sometimes things get worse before they get better. But hang in there. Things will get better!

Think of road construction. In order to get smooth roads, we have to deal with cracked concrete, orange safety cones, and bothersome detours. Likewise, clearing the clutter from your heart takes time; it's a process.

As you pray and take action, you will find more peace and freedom. You'll feel lighter, as if a weight has been lifted from you. Mostly, you will be making room for new things. And when you do, you never know what surprises God may have in store for you.

A Lesson from Autumn Leaves

There's something about the brilliant colors of autumn leaves as green gives way to flaming red, vibrant yellow, or amber orange. Before the first snow falls, each leaf wafts to the ground, and only the barren tree branches remain. It's a shedding of sorts. For a season, it looks as if the gnarly trees will be empty forever. But just as sure as spring comes, tiny buds appear, lush green leaves form, and mighty maples, oaks, and aspens come to life again. Old leaves fall; new growth comes. In your quest to clean up your house or restore your inner life, remember that there is a reason for release and a season for renewal.

CLEANSE MY HEART, LORD

Let us draw near to God with a sincere heart and with the full assurance that faith brings, having our hearts sprinkled to cleanse us from a guilty conscience and having our bodies washed with pure water.

Hebrews 10:22

Lord, I humbly come before you. My life is a mess right now, and I need your help. You know all the circumstances, and you know how I feel. I ask for forgiveness of my sins and wrongdoings. I am sorry. Please cleanse me from the inside out. I want to be right with you. By faith I believe that you take away my guilt and shame. Thank you. I ask in Jesus's mighty name. Amen.

HELP ME LET GO OF WHAT'S HOLDING ME BACK

Therefore, since we are surrounded by such a great cloud of witnesses, let us throw off everything that hinders and the sin that so easily entangles. And let us run with perseverance the race marked out for us.

Hebrews 12:1

Lord, sometimes I feel like there's a ball and chain around my ankle. I want to be free, but something holds me back. Give me the strength and courage to focus my eyes on you, knowing that you have the power to help me let go and release what's holding me back. It's time. I want to clear the clutter from my heart and make room for better things. I surrender. Let me run this race with you! I ask in Jesus's name. Amen.

REBUILD MY LIFE

Can they bring the stones back to life from those heaps of rubble—burned as they are?

Nehemiah 4:2

Lord, my life feels like it's in ruins. What a mess! I can relate to Nehemiah as he stood among piles of rocks and charred remains after his beloved city burned to the ground. There is so much rubble in my life too. But he didn't give up, and you did not give up on him. He trusted you, enlisted help, and got to work. Bring me back to life, Lord. Rebuild me. I ask in Jesus's name. Amen.

RESCUE ME

He rescued me from my powerful enemy,
    from my foes, who were too strong for me.
They confronted me in the day of my disaster,
    but the LORD was my support.

2 Samuel 22:18–19

Lord, I praise you. Thank you for saving me from my enemies. They may not be warriors who shoot arrows, but people—even friends— sling verbal arrows of hurtful words into my heart. My situation seems impossible, Lord, but you are stronger than any adversary. May the "day of my disaster" turn into days of delight. Near you, I am safe. And here I will stay. In Jesus's name. Amen.

GETTING MY PRIORITIES IN ORDER

Love the LORD your God with all your heart and with all your soul and with all your strength.

Deuteronomy 6:5

Lord, so many things clamor for my attention in life. Often, I feel pulled in a hundred different directions. How can I get it all done? Help me to remember to put you first. I love you, and I truly want to love you with all my heart—with everything I am. You are my first priority, and from that everything else flows. I believe you will direct my footsteps each day and fill me with peace and contentment as I trust you. In Jesus's name. Amen.

THE WORLD IS A MESS

In this world you will have trouble. But take heart! I have overcome the world.

John 16:33

Lord, our world is a mess. Yes, there are so many good things, but my heart breaks for the global issues of poverty, homelessness, war, and lack of safety and resources for so many. Give me eyes to see beyond my own pain and help me to pray for the needs of others. You are greater than the greatest needs. You are the Overcomer! Come, Lord, and bring healing. I ask, believing in Jesus's name. Amen.

4

When You're Disappointed

Prayers for Encouragement

Then you will know that I am the LORD;
those who hope in me will not be
disappointed.

Isaiah 49:23

Rob was frustrated. A hailstorm had ruined his roof, and the insurance company wasn't paying enough to get a new one. Marie was betrayed by someone she thought was a loyal friend, and she's still reeling from it. Keisha, who's been trying—off and on—to lose weight for years, is continually discouraged. Life can be disappointing.

Dashed hopes and thwarted dreams come in all shapes and sizes, and they're always painful. It's normal to feel sad or upset when bad things happen; God designed us with emotions. But we must deal with our disappointments so little hurts don't turn into large ones. Disappointment can spiral quickly into despair or depression if we don't get ahold of our thought life.

Dealing with Disappointment

When you don't get the job you wanted, when your husband forgets your birthday, or when your loan application is denied, how do you handle your disappointment? Do you sulk, or do you stand strong on the promises of God? Remember, you have a choice.

What you tell yourself matters. Disappointment is a part of life. Whether they're big hurts or little ones, it's what you do with your pain that determines how you will move forward. What are you saying to yourself about what's happened? Are you feeling hopeless and thinking, *I'm never going to find a job?* Or hopeful and thinking, *I guess that wasn't the right job for me. God has something better suited to my skills. I will bounce back?*

Don't mull; release disappointments. My mother used to say that garbage needs to be taken out at least once a week, and so does the garbage in your heart. When you hold on to frustration, resentment, or discouragement, it can fester inside. Instead, feel your feelings and then release your pain. The best way to do that is in prayer; talk to God about how you feel and what happened. He hears, he sees, and he truly cares.

Wait on God to make things right. When disappointment comes, you may think it's the end of the story. But it may not be. That's where discernment and having the wisdom to wait come into play. Waiting strengthens your trust muscles, teaching you to depend solely on God, not your circumstances. There's a popular saying, "Don't place a period where God has placed a comma." This disappointment may be the final curtain, or it may simply be an intermission, a time to wait on God.

My friend Barbara had been dating Steve for more than a year, and while he'd brought up the topic of marriage, she was uncertain about some things she felt she needed in a godly husband. So she ended the relationship. Hard as it was, Barbara held to her trust in God to make things right. Whether they got back together or not, she knew that God had his best in mind for her. She closed the door on the relationship and chose to get on with her life.

Unbeknownst to Barbara, God was doing an amazing transformational work in Steve's heart about God's design for marriage and other things. One Saturday afternoon, Barbara was praying and felt the Holy Spirit tell her to be open to Steve if he were to call, to "drop the drawbridge to the fortress." She didn't think he would contact her. She thought it was over—they both did. But God had different plans.

That same Saturday afternoon, Steve called Barbara from a mountaintop where he'd been praying and listening to God. Steve didn't think she'd pick up the phone, but she did. They began to connect in an entirely new way. After a time apart that drew them solely to God and not each other, they both felt that God was reuniting them. They knew that the Lord had put them back together and that he had a plan for their relationship. Shortly after that they got engaged and two months later were married.

Trust God in the silent times. He is working, even in the spaces.

Get a fresh perspective. Ask yourself, *How can I view this situation differently?* Perhaps you need a fresh perspective. Just as flying high in an airplane helps you see the bigger picture of the earth below, getting a new viewpoint on your circumstances can help you feel better. Ask God to open your eyes to the truth about what's happening so you can see more clearly how to pray and what to do. We all go through emotional growing pains that serve to make us stronger on the inside. Ask yourself, *What can I learn from this situation? How can my faith be strengthened here?*

Don't let your disappointment make you disillusioned with God. If you've been disappointed, you may feel like God doesn't care or that he's abandoned you. Nothing could be further from the truth. Don't let your circumstances rob you of the unchanging truths that God is wiser than you and that he knows best.

Romans 8:28 says, "And we know that in all things God works for the good of those who love him, who have been called according to his purpose." All things? Even this painful disappointment? Yes, even this. We don't know how or when, but God promises to work all things together for a higher and better purpose. That's where trust comes in. How many times have you been able to see in hindsight where God was leading?

After being unemployed for months, I finally landed a position that was suited to my skills in writing and editing. Only then could I look back and see how God was saving this destination for me; the other jobs I didn't get were stepping-stones to lead me to this place. Every no was one step closer to the ultimate yes.

Lift up your eyes. When discouragement or disappointments have you down, it's time to look up. Psalm 121:1–2 says, "I lift up my eyes to the mountains—where does my help come from? My help comes from the LORD, the Maker of heaven and earth." Instead of looking all around at your circumstances or looking down in despair, choose to look to the one who has the power to do something about your situation. He will lift you up.

Deal and heal. Unless you remove dandelions by the roots, their little yellow heads will keep popping up in your yard. In the same way, only when you get to the root of your issues will you begin to rid the landscape of your life of irritations such as constant regret or bitterness. As you deal with your emotions— feeling your feelings, not ignoring them, and surrendering your pain to God in prayer—you will begin to heal. The power of prayer gets to the root of the issue because God heals from the inside out. As you pray, God changes your discouragement to encouragement or your sadness to joy, and a much more joyful self emerges.

Prayer changes things, and it changes you. As you pray about your disappointments, be encouraged and remember the one to whom you pray. God Almighty is all-powerful and full of more strength and wisdom than you can ever comprehend. He can take care of your situation.

Our times are in his hands.

A Lesson from Wildflowers

After a relationship breakup a few years ago, I went hiking in Evergreen, Colorado. My emotions were still raw from the unexpected severing of emotional ties, so I had my eyes more on the path than on the beauty of the forest around me. For some reason, I looked to the right of the trail and spotted a tree stump. The sawed-off tree reminded me of my own miserable situation: broken and purposeless. It was no longer the tall and beautiful tree it was once. I looked more closely, and to my surprise I saw tiny, colorful wildflowers growing from the center of the damaged stump—a surprise of beauty, a symbol of new life and growth. In a single moment, a spark of renewed hope lit inside me. Maybe, just maybe, there was life after loss. It was the start of my new beginning.

STRENGTH IN DISCOURAGEMENT

> Be strong and take heart,
> all you who hope in the Lord.
>
> Psalm 31:24

Lord, it's been a long, hard road for me lately. I'm tired. You know my heart, and you see how disappointed I've been in my circumstances. Please strengthen me and give me new hope. Help me to remember that my hope is in you—the Creator and Sustainer of the universe and of my life. Nothing is too big or too small for you to handle. In my weakness, be my true strength. In Jesus's mighty name. Amen.

PRESSING ON!

Brothers and sisters, I do not consider myself yet to have taken hold of it. But one thing I do: Forgetting what is behind and straining toward what is ahead, I press on toward the goal to win the prize for which God has called me heavenward in Christ Jesus.

Philippians 3:13–14

Lord, help me to be a "one thing" person as I leave the past in the past and look toward a brighter future with you. I'm not perfect; far from it. But you are giving me a vision of a life better than I ever could have imagined. Show me what is holding me back, and help me to release it and press on! One step at a time, face forward, I walk on with you. Thank you for loving me. In Jesus's name. Amen.

I NEED MORE POWER

Be strong and courageous. Do not be afraid or discouraged because of the king of Assyria and the vast army with him, for there is a greater power with us than with him. With him is only the arm of flesh, but with us is the LORD our God to help us and to fight our battles.

2 Chronicles 32:7–8

Lord, I feel like I have so many battles to fight each day, like discouragement and conflict with others. You know my needs. Just as you gave words of encouragement to your people long ago when an army intended to siege their city, Jerusalem, speak words of encouragement to me. You are with me, and you promised to help me fight all my battles. I believe you. I trust you. And I ask for your greater power to help me. In Jesus's name. Amen.

HELP MY FEAR AND DOUBT

He said to them, "Why are you troubled, and why do doubts rise in your minds?"

Luke 24:38

Lord, I've been living in fear and doubt lately, and I am sorry. I've been listening to people who tear me down, but you want to encourage me with your unchanging truth. You say, "Believe me," and yet I chase after other things or people who I think will satisfy my longings. But they always leave me wanting more. Forgive me for forgetting that you are my satisfaction. You are first. May your peace restore me. In Jesus's name. Amen.

BRING BACK THE HOPE

Then you will know that I am the LORD;
    those who hope in me will not be disappointed.

Isaiah 49:23

Lord, some days are really hard. I've been disappointed and discouraged lately, and I just can't seem to shake it. Please bring my hope back again. Help me to see with new eyes the light at the end of the darkness. Help me choose to put my trust in you and not my circumstances. I need to focus on the truth; I put the center of my attention on you, not all the chaos and confusion swirling around me. Renew my hope, Lord. I ask in Jesus's name. Amen.

ENCOURAGE ME, LORD

You, LORD, hear the desire of the afflicted;
    you encourage them, and you listen to their cry.

Psalm 10:17

Lord, thank you that you hear me when I pray. It makes me happy to know that you listen and pay attention to each word I'm saying. It makes me feel special to know that you truly care. Will you shower your love and encouragement on me today? I need a waterfall of blessings to wash over me. Hydrate me, refresh me, and renew me, Lord. I am so grateful for all you are and all you do. I love you. In Jesus's name. Amen.

5

When You're Depressed

Prayers for Wild Hope and Renewed Joy

Why, my soul, are you downcast?
Why so disturbed within me?
Put your hope in God,
for I will yet praise him,
my Savior and my God.

Psalm 42:5

One January night, an emotionally distraught seventeen-year-old girl lay across train tracks near her Midwestern home. The weight of trauma in her young life seemed too much to bear. She wanted a way out; she wanted the pain to end. An oncoming train careening toward her couldn't stop in time, and thirty-three freight cars rolled over her body.

But that was not the end of the story. When the train finally stopped, Kristen realized she was still alive! She had survived, but her legs had been cut off. Her battle was far from over.

Her name is Kristen Jane Anderson, and the story of her amazing recovery from physical and emotional pain is told in her book, *Life, in Spite of Me* (with Tricia Goyer). God worked a miracle in the young girl's life that night. And years later when she met Bill, one of the paramedics who treated her, she would learn more about what had really happened.

The night of her suicide attempt, Bill told Kristen, they tried to bring in a Flight for Life helicopter, but it was too foggy. "Instead they did something I hadn't seen before and I haven't seen happen since. They radioed in and had all the intersections between where you were and the hospital blocked. A drive that normally would have taken forty-five minutes took only eight minutes. I think we were all so surprised you were alive that we wanted to make sure we did all we could."[1]

"God kept you here for a reason, Kristen," he concluded.[2]

Someone you know may be experiencing depression right now: your next-door neighbor, a co-worker, the new person in your small group, someone you care about—even you. Depression has many faces. We all feel sad, hopeless, or down in the dumps at times; that's part of life, and it's normal for a short period of time. But when those feelings won't go away and despondency is severe, it is called major depression.

Surprisingly, more than one in twenty Americans twelve years of age and older suffer from depression, according to the Centers for Disease Control.[3] Here's how the CDC defines it:

> *Major depression* is a clinical syndrome of at least five symptoms that cluster together, last for at least 2 weeks, and cause impairment in functioning. Mood symptoms include depressed, sad, or irritable mood, loss of interest in usual activities, inability to experience pleasure, feelings of guilt or worthlessness, and thoughts of death or suicide. Cognitive symptoms include inability to concentrate and difficulty making decisions. Physical symptoms include fatigue, lack of energy, feeling either restless or slowed down, and changes in sleep, appetite, and activity levels.[4]

Life on the Edge

Sometimes instead of living the dream, you feel like you're living the nightmare. Your son overdosed on drugs. You got fired. Your wife or husband just passed away. You're disappointed with how your life has turned out. You never planned on being divorced, or overweight, or childless. You wanted a peaceful life, and your job is extremely stressful. You may be asking yourself, *How did I get here? How will things ever change?*

No matter what your situation, there is hope. As with Kristen, God has you here for a reason. He longs for you to live with purpose and power. But how do you keep on going when you feel so desperate?

During a hard time in my life years ago, I had a picture in my head of living life on the edge; I felt as if I were hanging over a cliff with only one hand on the ledge. Depleted, isolated, and depressed, I was barely hanging on. But as I prayed and trusted God—even as I wept and wondered—things began to change. Bit by bit, relief came. God strengthened me as I prayed. Over time, I felt as if I were hanging on with two hands. Then Jesus lifted me up from the ledge, and I was standing on solid ground. Finally, we walked away, and "ledge living" was but a distant memory.

Standing strong in hard times isn't just for other people. You can be an overcomer. You may feel as if you're living in a black-and-white world, but God wants to bring back the living color. As you learn to believe God and bask in his presence, you'll discover wild hope—hope beyond your wildest imagination.

Believing God

For a long time I didn't know the difference between *believing in* God and *believing* God. I knew I believed in God, that he existed and that he did an awesome, redeeming work when he sent his

Son, Jesus, to die and rise again so we could be forgiven and be with him forever in heaven. But believing God to keep his promises and be true to his Word? That was another story.

Beth Moore's *Believing God* Bible study helped me learn that "God is so much more than we have yet acknowledged and experienced. He is capable of tremendously more than we have witnessed. . . . We see so little primarily because we believe him for so little."[5]

Oftentimes, when we've been disappointed by our earthly parents, we project that same quality onto God. We think he will break his promises too. But he doesn't. Maybe the fact that others have let you down is keeping you from believing God will come through for you. Some people break their promises, but God always keeps his; he is the ultimate Promise Keeper. What God says is worthy and true. "God is not human, that he should lie, not a human being, that he should change his mind. Does he speak and then not act? Does he promise and not fulfill?" (Num. 23:19). Instead of doubting, you can choose to believe God's promises in the Bible and believe that he is at work in your life, even when you cannot see it.

Think about this. If a tourist drove through Colorado Springs on a foggy day, she wouldn't be able to see Pikes Peak; she may not believe the mountain is really there. But as a resident, I know it's there; I see it every day. I know with certainty that when the clouds clear, America's Mountain will be standing strong. Likewise, when we cannot *see* the way out of our foggy lives, we can choose to *believe* God is still here. Always here. He knows what is ahead even when we do not, and he is at work behind the scenes.

Choose to believe God is working all things together for the good in your life despite circumstances, or feelings, or what the world says. And even if you don't feel that way right away, the feelings will follow.

Believing God means you also take action. James 2:17 tells us that "faith by itself, if it is not accompanied by action, is dead."

One step at a time, one moment at a time, you move forward—even if it's something as simple as eating breakfast. Then get dressed. Then make a list of what you're going to do today. You're building momentum as one step leads to another. And when life tries to drag you down, you make new choices and keep telling yourself the truth.

Basking in His Presence

We are changed by God's love, and we are changed by his truth. You can tell yourself the truth in many ways. When you read the Bible, God's truth in written form, consider reading the words out loud. When you pray—which is talking with God—you may choose to speak out loud instead of praying silently to yourself. Or write your prayers in a journal or notebook. Remember and record the good things he's done and how he's come through for you in the past. Read the psalms for healing words of hope during hard times and periods of discouragement. Like Psalm 32:7: "You are my hiding place; you will protect me from trouble and surround me with songs of deliverance." Remember that the Lord wants to spend time with you. He wants you to linger, to hang out, to bask in his presence.

Think of the most beautiful full moon you've seen. Perhaps it's a harvest moon hanging low in the October night sky. The moon reflects the light of the sun because it "basks" in its brightness. And in the dark of night, it shines brightly. Likewise, as we bask in the light of the Son, Jesus Christ—as we spend time abiding—his light shines brighter through us.

Having Wild Hope

Wild hope means hoping even when you feel you haven't got a chance. It is daring to believe that God will come through for you even in your toughest times. A different life may seem like a distant dream right now, but as you take small steps of faith, things will begin to change. God may not answer your prayers in the exact same way he's answered mine; he will meet your needs in the way that suits his best purposes for your life.

It just may surprise you who (or what) God will use to bring relief to your situation. It may be something tangible like a hug from a friend or an unexpected check in the mail. Liberation may come through acceptance of the situation or forgiving someone who's wronged you.

Believe God, bask in his presence, and pray, expecting things to change. Then one day you will begin to feel something unusual: joy. Darkness will begin to flee as the sunshine of hope rises in your heart like the dawn of a new day.

Dare to believe that the one who can do anything is at work even now restoring you and rebuilding your life.

A Lesson from a Summer Storm

It was a hot July day, and from my patio door I could see ominous gray clouds gathering. It looked like the end of the world. Suddenly, the sky released pelting rain. Lightning cracked like gunfire, and thunder rolled and rolled. Hours passed. Finally, the clouds broke, revealing a luminous blue sky. Bright sunshine sparkled on wet grass, creating dew diamonds. It was clear again—so clear. Sometimes life feels like a tumultuous summer storm. It's dark and uncertain, and the sadness doesn't seem to budge. But thankfully, storms pass. Just as a strong wind clears away clouds, the Holy Spirit blows a fresh and purposeful wind of hope through your soul storm. After the rain, sunshine; after life's turbulent storms, renewed calm and joy.

HEAR MY CRY FOR HELP

> Hear my prayer, Lord,
> > listen to my cry for help;
> > do not be deaf to my weeping.

Psalm 39:12

Lord, it feels like a storm in my heart, a hurricane of emotions swirling about. I am so sad; I feel defeated. Where has my hope gone? I can't even form words to let you know how I really feel. Yet here I am. Thank you that you hear my cries, even my unformed words. Please help me. Please heal me. Be near me. You are my strong hope, and I pray, believing. In Jesus's mighty name. Amen.

RENEW MY STRENGTH

> You wearied yourself by such going about,
> > but you would not say, "It is hopeless."
> You found renewal of your strength,
> > and so you did not faint.

Isaiah 57:10

Lord, I just want to cry. I am so tired of my miserable life. Please heal me from this depression. I don't want to feel hopeless; I want to be hopeful. But I don't have the strength to muster up hope. Pour your strength in me; fill me anew. Help me to move forward with courage, knowing you are with me and you are for me. My times are in your good hands. In Jesus's name. Amen.

PUSH BACK THE DARKNESS

> For you were once darkness, but now you are light in the
> Lord. Live as children of light (for the fruit of the light
> consists in all goodness, righteousness and truth).

Ephesians 5:8–9

Lord, I come confidently and boldly before you, and I ask in the name and power of Jesus that you would push back the darkness in my life.

61

Let your light of truth overcome the awful things that seek to undo me. Your name has authority! And I choose to stand on the unchanging promises of God. With you darkness flees. Help me to live with more peace. In Jesus's name I pray. Amen.

FINDING LIFE AGAIN

I will not die but live,
 and will proclaim what the LORD has done.

Psalm 118:17

Lord, this has been one of the lowest places I've been for a long time. Sometimes I've felt like I wanted to die. But I didn't. Your hand was on me. You, Lord, saved and protected me. And now, I'm beginning to see the dawn of a new day in the landscape of my life. I have glimpses of new hope. Lord, I want to live! I want to be able to tell others how great you are and all you have done for me! You are my Wild Hope, and I thank you and praise you. In Jesus's holy name. Amen.

GOD'S POWER IN ME

And if the Spirit of him who raised Jesus from the dead is living in you, he who raised Christ from the dead will also give life to your mortal bodies because of his Spirit who lives in you.

Romans 8:11

Lord, I have been depressed for a long time. I need your help to get off the couch, to change my thoughts, and to heal my life. Your Word tells me that when I believe in you, your power is alive in me. It's the same power that raised Jesus Christ from the dead! Please help me to do what I cannot do in my own strength. Lead me to find purpose, joy, and love again. When I am holding on to Jesus, I am holding on to hope. Be my Wild Hope—amazing and good, more than I can ask for or imagine. I put my trust in you. In Jesus's name. Amen.

LIFT ME UP, LORD

But you, Lord, are a shield around me,
  my glory, the One who lifts my head high.

Psalm 3:3

How can I thank you, Lord, for lifting up my head—and my life—when I have been so downcast? It has been a dark and discouraging time, but I feel your protection. You are my defense against the enemies of fear, doubt, and dread. You are carrying me. Like a shepherd carries a lost sheep, you hold me close. I praise you, Lord, thankful that you care so much for me. In Jesus's name. Amen.

WALKING BY FAITH

For we live by faith, not by sight.

2 Corinthians 5:7

Lord, here I am coming to you for help. I don't know what to do. I don't know what's going to happen in my situation. Please show me the way. Yet even when I cannot see, you tell me to have faith. Lord, increase my faith! I choose to believe you are my Helper and Healer. You're all I've got. But you're everything. Your love toward me is constant—on cloudy days and sunny days. On that I will rely. In Jesus's name. Amen.

6

When You Feel Insecure

Prayers for Confidence

It is God who arms me with strength
and keeps my way secure.

2 Samuel 22:33

My new friend Julie told me recently that she grew up as a very insecure girl, not the adventurous type at all. She suffered verbal abuse for years from classmates. And her father, whom she loved dearly, passed away when she was only thirteen. Yet here she was dangling from a harness over the edge of a cliff, rappelling in the early hours of a warm July day in Colorado.

Halfway down the mountain, she paused. Her big brown eyes scanned the scenic beauty around her—a cloudless blue sky and morning sunshine glistening on Mount Princeton. She pondered the journey she'd been on for the past few years that led her to this moment. *Who is this person I've become?* she asked herself.

A few years ago, you couldn't have paid her to go near athletic activities, let alone lead the charge in daring escapades such as the leap of faith on a ropes course or skydiving. Now, she couldn't get enough of them.

In the past few years, Julie had moved from rural Oklahoma to LA to work with some of Hollywood's elite. She'd learned to boldly share her faith, and most recently, she'd left friends and family to move to Colorado Springs to work for an incredible ministry.

Julie smiled. She was different—Christ had changed her. "What an incredible God we serve who can change us so much," Julie said. "Each day he changes us to become more and more like him."

How did Julie get rid of her deep insecurities and transform into this new person she barely recognizes?

Because of her past, said Julie, "I was always a bit leery of trusting the Lord fully. As much as I would try to rely on my heavenly Father, when a difficult situation would strike, insecurity would invade, and I'd be frightened all over again." Then she'd run to her prayer closet and pray until God gave her the strength to emerge once more.

A newfound confidence began to surface in Julie's life when she discovered God's truths in Romans 8. The Message reads this way:

> Those who think they can do it on their own end up obsessed with measuring their own moral muscle but never get around to exercising it in real life. Those who trust God's action in them find that God's Spirit is in them—living and breathing God! (vv. 5–6)

Julie reminded me that the resurrection life we receive from God is not a timid, grave-tending life. It's adventurously expectant. Now she greets God in her prayer time with a childlike, "What's next, Papa?" As God's Spirit touches your spirit, he confirms who you really are—a son or daughter of the King (see Rom. 8:15–16).

Why Are We Insecure?

A lack of confidence or anxiety arises in our lives for many reasons. I know many women who feel self-conscious because they've gained weight or have bad skin. Perhaps you're a new mom who's hesitant about anything baby-related and wonder, *Am I doing this right?* I remember when I was a new manager and felt inadequate for the monumental tasks on my to-do list. Certainly, insecurity can manifest itself in many ways.

Often, we feel we are not good enough. You may feel invisible or embarrassed because you don't believe you have enough education, enough beauty, enough money, or enough of whatever it is you think you need to be to please others. You question things incessantly: *Does he still love me? Can I really do this job? Will anyone like me at this new small group? Are people staring at me?*

Sometimes we assume what others think when we don't really know; we project our own insecurity onto a situation. On some level, it's normal to question things. But if we obsess and stress about our insecurities all the time, we surely need relief.

You may be highly sensitive to the comments of others because of your wounded past. Do you feel unworthy? Perhaps it's because you've experienced large losses in life. You may have grown up in a home of utter chaos and inconsistent loving. You may have felt unloved or rejected. If you have been abused or abandoned (physically or emotionally), you may have no real foundation for secure love—no basement on which the building blocks of confidence and true worth stand strong. You don't know what nurturing or comfort feels like, and that can affect your level of confidence in the future.

As a child, if you did not receive affirmation and encouragement from grown-ups (parents, teachers, coaches, and others) to help you build a strong sense of identity, you may have a distorted perception of yourself or of God.

Distorted Images

A lack of confidence and its opposite, pride, comprise both ends of the spectrum. Is there a balance somewhere in between for a healthy self-image and a confident spirit? Consider a true sense of self-esteem from my book *When Love Ends and the Ice Cream Carton Is Empty*:

> Perhaps you've seen a woman who thinks she is "all that." Her smugness and conceit is contrasted with the person who has low self-esteem: she thinks she is "none of that." She focuses more on her mistakes instead of what she does right. She is often sad or fearful, and her insecurity prevents her from speaking up, taking chances, or moving forward. Whether it's too high or too low, ask yourself if your assessment of your self is accurate. Ask God to give you insight.
>
> A woman with a healthy self-esteem respects herself. She feels secure and worthwhile because of what God says about her. She has confidence in relationships and in life and generally more joy. She knows she has significance; she matters. With her sense of worth and value intact, she sits up straight and walks tall. Her head up, this confident woman is friendly, gentle, and kind. She makes eye contact when she speaks, and she doesn't constantly apologize for everything she says or does.[1]

Living Your True Identity

We all have reasons for feeling insecure. But we don't have to stay there; we have choices. Instead of living in insecurity, you can choose to live "in security." That means you are secure in your identity because you know whose you are. And as you uncover the truth about what God says about you, you can be confident in who you are. What does God say about your true identity? You are:

Accepted by God—Romans 15:7

Blessed—Matthew 5:2–12

The bride of Christ—Revelation 19:7

A child of God—John 1:12

Chosen—Ephesians 1:11

A citizen of heaven—Philippians 3:20

A friend—John 15:15

His co-worker—2 Corinthians 6:1

His handiwork—Ephesians 2:10

The light of the world—Matthew 5:14

Loved dearly—Colossians 3:12

Victorious—1 Corinthians 15:57

Self-Confidence or God-Confidence?

In what or whom are you putting your trust? Are you relying on your sense of self or your idea of true beauty from women's magazines, Hollywood actors, or what other people say? If so, your self-esteem will quickly crumble. Confidence is about much more than how a person looks on the outside. God sees things another way. First Samuel 16:7 says, "The LORD does not look at the things people look at. People look at the outward appearance, but the LORD looks at the heart."

Instead of relying on what others say or finding confidence in yourself, you can build God-confidence by remembering that *he can do what you cannot*. In other words, focus on what he can do through you rather than your own limited resources.

One of the most memorable characters in the Bible lacked confidence. Remember the scene at the burning bush? God called to Moses and asked him to go to Pharaoh, the head of Egypt, to get the people of Israel out of that country. Instead of thinking,

God can, he fretted, *Can I?* He said, "Please send someone else" (Exod. 4:13). He felt unqualified; he wasn't eloquent enough and was slow of speech (see 4:10). Moses wasn't looking at what God could do; he was fearful of what he was *not*.

Generations later we read that story and wonder why Moses was so uncertain. In that conversation alone, God showed him three miracles! Moses saw a bush that burned but did not burn up, a staff that turned into a snake and back again, and his own hand turn leprous and then healthy again. God even said, "I will be with you" (3:12). After all that you'd think Moses would believe. But he doubted again and again. Yet God used him mightily.

When we feel ill-equipped or inadequate, that's the time to rely on God and what he can do through us. We can be secure when we know the one in whom we can put our confidence. "It is God who arms me with strength and keeps my way secure" (2 Sam. 22:33).

Immerse yourself in God's truth and love, and you will find insecurity fading and confidence building. When we see with the eyes of Christ, we see who we really are.

A Lesson from a Geode

You may have heard the expression "Don't judge a book by its cover." That popular saying couldn't be truer than for a geode. This melon-shaped rock, dull on the outside, is generally brown and nondescript. But crack it open and you will see on the inside an extraordinary display of colorful quartz crystals and calcite, handmade by the Creator of the universe. Unexpected splendor!

Some days you may feel like the outside of a geode—plain and ordinary—but the truth is that there is a treasure within. When Christ lives in you, he can give you confidence on the inside—where it counts. Then when life's pressures come and you feel broken in two, God can reveal the beauty of brokenness.

70

FACING FORWARD

I keep my eyes always on the LORD.
    With him at my right hand, I will not be shaken.
Therefore my heart is glad and my tongue rejoices;
    my body also will rest secure.

Psalm 16:8–9

Lord, when I look at circumstances around me, I get all worked up. I feel insecure and unsure. I don't know what to do. So I choose to keep my eyes on you—face forward, not looking to the left or the right. Help me to stay focused. I am so glad I can trust you with my heart. I feel safe with you. Empower me and embolden me, Lord. Thank you for helping me to be a more confident person. In Jesus's name. Amen.

FEAR NOT

So we say with confidence, "The Lord is my helper; I will not be afraid. What can mere mortals do to me?"

Hebrews 13:6

Lord, sometimes I wonder what other people think of me. I doubt whether I am enough or if I am adequate for the tasks at hand each day. I really want to do my best and be all that you want me to be in this life. I know I cannot do it on my own. Please give me God-confidence, not self-confidence, because I know that you can do greater things through me than I could ever conjure up myself. You are my Helper, my Healer, my wise Counsel. With you I stand strong. In Jesus's name. Amen.

WHAT IS MY CONFIDENCE BASED ON?

But blessed is the one who trusts in the LORD,
    whose confidence is in him.

Jeremiah 17:7

Lord, so many times I have based my confidence on my own abilities, on what my friends think, on what I hear in the media. Why do I care so much about the opinions of others? Help me to block distorted thinking that says I have to be something I am not. Help me to dwell in the truth and to put my trust in you. When I know I am yours, I can make better choices from a solid bedrock of total acceptance. You are my sure foundation. In Jesus's name. Amen.

TREASURES IN HEAVEN

So do not throw away your confidence; it will be richly rewarded.

Hebrews 10:35

Lord, I feel like I am learning more each day about how to be a confident person. Sometimes I forget all you have given me, the assurance of your love, acceptance, and provision. Please forgive me for walking past the truth and settling for lies and half-truths that the world throws my way. Help me to hold fast and cling to the treasures you give me: I am your beloved. I am your child. Your power and strength course through me to enable me to say the right things and stand strong. Help me to hold on to my beliefs and hold on to hope, knowing that one day I will be rewarded in heaven. I ask in Jesus's name. Amen.

BY GRACE ALONE

Let us then approach God's throne of grace with confidence, so that we may receive mercy and find grace to help us in our time of need.

Hebrews 4:16

Lord, I love you so much. Thank you for providing a way for me to come before you with confidence, not with hesitation or fear. You are welcoming, and you want me to come to you anytime—day or night. Here, in the comfort of your love and in the holiness of your justice, I find help. You know my needs, and I ask for your grace—not because of what I have done but because of who I am: your child. Thank you for your goodness and grace. In Jesus's name. Amen.

AUTHENTIC BEAUTY

Charm is deceptive, and beauty is fleeting;
  but a woman who fears the LORD is to be praised.

Proverbs 31:30

Lord, please help me to see myself the way you see me. Confirm in my life what I have heard and let me experience it. Your Word says that I am your child. Because I serve the King of kings, I am a princess. You created me; I was your idea! Despite how I look or don't look, despite how I feel or don't feel, your Word stands strong and true. I choose to believe and bask in your truth and your unending love for me. In Jesus's name. Amen.

YOU ARE MY FORTRESS

Truly he is my rock and my salvation;
  he is my fortress, I will never be shaken.

Psalm 62:2

Lord, so many things in life try to shake me up. I feel like people expect me to be so many things—at home and at work. I just don't know if I can do it. What if I disappoint them? What if I can't do it all? I doubt my abilities, and my confidence is shaky. Help me to remember that you are my rock, my strength. You are the one I can run to when I feel my world crumbling. I cling to you, Lord. In Jesus's name. Amen.

GOD IS MY HELPER

When all our enemies heard about this, all the surrounding nations were afraid and lost their self-confidence, because they realized that this work had been done with the help of our God.

Nehemiah 6:16

Lord, you are so good! Centuries ago, you helped Nehemiah when he faced opposition while reconstructing the broken walls of Jerusalem. Because his enemies saw that you were his helper in this massive task, they were frightened and doubted. But he completed the task and stood strong. Today, you still help those in need, and I am so glad you help me. No matter what, you are mighty to save and to help me in my times of need. Thank you! Replenish me, Lord. May your confidence flow through me so I can have the strength I need today. In Jesus's name. Amen.

7

When You Feel Fearful

Prayers for Courage

So do not fear, for I am with you;
    do not be dismayed, for I am your God.
I will strengthen you and help you;
    I will uphold you with my righteous right hand.

Isaiah 41:10

It's not always easy to listen to the evening news. Tonight I learned that the Dow plunged hundreds of points, thirty American troops were killed in Afghanistan (twenty-two of them Navy Seals), and severe famine is raging in the horn of Africa. One woman said she had walked for three months just to get to the refugee camp. Think of where you were three months ago.

On the one hand, you may feel compassion; on the other, numbness or fear. *What is this world coming to?* Whether it is over world events or personal issues, fear comes in all sizes.

What Are We Afraid Of?

In an uncertain economy, many people wonder about layoffs and budget cuts. *Will my job be the next one to go? Will we lose the house? What will happen to my shrinking retirement savings?*

Last year I was unemployed for six months when the company I worked for had nationwide layoffs, and it was a test of faith to live on unemployment benefits. Of course, I was grateful to have income of any kind, but it simply wasn't enough to live on if I wanted to pay bills *and* eat. Often, I wondered where the rest of the money would come from. When the human side of me felt fear creeping up, I chose to push past "there won't be enough" thoughts and pray for "more than enough." Time and again God answered my prayers through the help of generous friends who knew my desperate situation. Every month I wondered, and every month God came through.

My trust muscles were strengthened during that time as I learned that God was true to his Word. It's one thing to say, "I trust God" when things are going well; it's quite another to live it when you are literally down to your last dime.

Fear can be paralyzing. Oftentimes, worries and doubts stop us from taking action and having what we really want in life. Daryl, for instance, is so afraid of rejection that he hasn't asked a woman out in years. But he still desires to be married one day. Cassie creates amazing art on canvas but is terrified no one will like her work, so she never shows it to anyone.

When you are afraid, will you have fear or faith? Will you trust God or succumb to your fear? One phrase often used in the Bible is "do not fear" or "do not be afraid." Here are just a few examples (emphasis added in all verses):

Abram (who would later be named Abraham), when he learned that he would have as many offspring as the number of stars in the sky: "After this, the word of the LORD came to Abram in a vision: '*Do not be afraid*, Abram. I am your shield, your very great reward'" (Gen. 15:1).

Moses, when chased by Pharaoh's army: "Moses answered the people, '*Do not be afraid*. Stand firm and you will see the deliverance the LORD will bring you today. The Egyptians you see today you will never see again. The LORD will fight for you; you need only to be still'" (Exod. 14:13–14).

Joshua, who succeeded Moses, when he was about to lead the Israelite people into the Promised Land: "Have I not commanded you? Be strong and courageous. *Do not be afraid*; do not be discouraged, for the LORD your God will be with you wherever you go" (Josh. 1:9).

Joseph, before he married Mary, Jesus's mother: "But after he had considered this, an angel of the Lord appeared to him in a dream and said, 'Joseph son of David, *do not be afraid* to take Mary home as your wife, because what is conceived in her is from the Holy Spirit'" (Matt. 1:20).

I imagine most people would rightly be afraid if an angel appeared to them or they heard the audible voice of God. But it's what these ordinary people did after a fearful encounter that made a difference. Despite their fear, each of them pressed on, believing God and moving forward in faith. The same is true for you and me; we can decide what we will do with the fear we feel. We can learn to overcome by the power of God.

God Comes Through

I once heard about an American missionary family—a couple with children—whose village in Somalia was being attacked home by home. Rebels, without a hint of a moral compass, were looting and killing people. The family barely had time to run into the bedroom, shut the door, and huddle around the bed. Afraid for their lives, they prayed silently. They could hear the scuffle of feet on the other side of the bedroom door, and then silence.

Hours later, when they dared emerge from the bedroom, the family went outside and talked to someone who said the rebels had been caught. They learned that when the rebels were asked by the authorities why they didn't kill the missionary family, they replied, "We tried every door in that house. We didn't see that door." The family was spared because God had blocked the killers' eyes from seeing the very door behind which they were hiding, and they passed it by!

Overcoming Fear

How do you put aside worry and doubt? First, remember what God has done in the past—for you and for others. Recall how he has seen you through before and believe that he will again. Ask the Holy Spirit to help you do what you cannot do.

Fear says, "I cannot handle this situation." Faith says, "God can." When you surrender and let go of how you think things are supposed to be, they can begin to change. Trust that even though you can't see now how everything is going to work out, God knows. Store up inside you the truth about who God is as Protector, Helper, and Healer. He is stronger than any force that tries to come against you. God whispers, "Will you trust me? Will you believe I will take care of all your needs and calm your fears?"

Even as you trust, sometimes you need to stand and fight because your fear or panic could be a spiritual battle. Your enemy may not be an invading country or an attacker on the street. The number one enemy of humankind is the devil, and he is out to kill, steal, and destroy (see John 10:10). He wants to kill your hope, steal your joy, and destroy your life. Even though it may be hard to talk about, we need to know there is an enemy so we can fight against him. How do you stand and fight against an enemy you cannot see?

Remember, you are not alone. The Lord is with you always, and he will fight for you.

The plan is this: submit, resist, and win! James 4:7 states, "Submit yourselves, then, to God. Resist the devil, and he will flee from you." We are like spiritual firefighters as we "extinguish the flames" of our enemy with prayer. Ephesians 6:11–13 tells us more:

> Put on the full armor of God, so that you can take your stand against the devil's schemes. For our struggle is not against flesh and blood, but against the rulers, against the authorities, against the powers of this dark world and against the spiritual forces of evil in the heavenly realms. Therefore put on the full armor of God, so that when the day of evil comes, you may be able to stand your ground, and after you have done everything, to stand.

That's why prayer is so important. Even when you don't know what to say, start with, "Lord, teach me to pray." You may not say things perfectly, and that's okay. The attitude of your heart matters more than your words. Remember, you have the power of the Holy Spirit to intercede for you (see Rom. 8:26).

The living God hears and acts on your behalf. His power can change things, calm your fears, and get you out of terrible situations—or get you through them. Whether you choose to pray silently, speak out loud, or write your prayers in a journal, God receives the prayers of a sincere heart.

When it seems as if the world is falling apart, when your personal life feels like a hurricane in the Atlantic, or when you simply don't know what to do, the Lord is your steady anchor. In the storms of life, he is your safety, your security, your strength. Fear turns to courage and faith as you release control and hold fast to the one who will never let you go. Fear not, for the Lord is near. In hard times, in all times, Jesus is your peace.

We have this hope as an anchor for the soul, firm and secure. (Heb. 6:19)

A Lesson from a Well-Worn Footpath

Walking with fear and doubt is like walking a well-worn footpath. It may be a familiar trail, but it leads to a place of darkness and despair. Instead of staying on a path that leads to destruction in your thought life, you can choose to put up a "road closed" sign and take another way. God's way, the highway of hope, leads to courage and faith. This road calls you to come forth from the darkness and into the light. It may seem odd to choose faith over fear, but here you are never alone. God is with you, and the power of the Holy Spirit will help you through. It's time to be set free from fear and to live in freedom and faith. Feel the warm sun on your face as you choose a new path of walking in the light of truth—living by faith, not by sight. Courage lives here. Which road will you take? The choice is yours.

UNFAILING LOVE

Cast all your anxiety on him because he cares for you.

1 Peter 5:7

Lord, please help me. I carry so much worry and concern; they feel like heavy chains around me, such weight in my heart. Yet your Word says to "cast my anxiety" on you. Dare I trust you for the impossible? I am at a crossroads. I've carried these fears for so long, and I am tired. Here, Lord, I give you my problems. I ask for help. Take this heavy weight of fear and lighten my heart with new faith, deeper faith. I ask, believing in Jesus's name. Amen.

NEVER FORSAKEN

Have I not commanded you? Be strong and courageous. Do not be afraid; do not be discouraged, for the LORD your God will be with you wherever you go.

Joshua 1:9

Lord, so many times I am tempted to doubt. I worry and fear what will happen. Fortify me and help me to be strong and courageous despite my circumstances. Knowing that you are near all the time makes all the difference; it gives me peace. You promised to be with me always, no matter where I go. Thank you, Lord. Help me to remember that and to feel your close presence. In Jesus's name. Amen.

FOR PEACEFUL SLEEP

In peace I will lie down and sleep,
    for you alone, LORD,
    make me dwell in safety.

Psalm 4:8

Lord, thank you that despite the storms of fear that rage around me, you are my peace. Help me to release my worries, to drop them at the foot of the cross, knowing that you can handle what I cannot. You, precious Lord, are my safety; with you I am secure. Give me peace and sweet sleep as I put my trust in you. In Jesus's name. Amen.

WALKING BY FAITH

For we live by faith, not by sight.

2 Corinthians 5:7

Lord, it seems that when I rely on what I see, or think I see, I can become afraid. But you see with a different set of eyes. You see the bigger picture—the beginning, the middle, and the end. You know what I don't know. So when I am tempted to rely solely on the circumstances around me, I will choose to walk by faith. I can have peace because you, mighty God, have a plan. In Jesus's name. Amen.

STAND STRONG

Finally, be strong in the Lord and in his mighty power. Put on the full armor of God, so that you can take your stand against the devil's schemes. For our struggle is not against flesh and blood, but against the rulers, against the authorities, against the powers of this dark world and against the spiritual forces of evil in the heavenly realms.

Ephesians 6:10–12

Lord, I need strength. Sometimes my worries and fears come against me, and I feel so powerless, so overwhelmed. But you, Lord, are stronger than any force on this planet—above it or below it. Fight for me! Push back the darkness in the name and power of Jesus. Help me to put on the full armor of God. With you I am an overcomer! I choose to believe and trust you. In Jesus's name. Amen.

PROTECTED FROM HARM

But the Lord is faithful, and he will strengthen you and protect you from the evil one.

2 Thessalonians 3:3

Lord, I am so glad that you are the strongest power in the universe. When things try to come against me, help me to remember that I am protected from harm and evil and I can call on Jesus's name. You protect me. You are my shield against the arrows of other people's hurt toward me or the evil one's lies. As I draw near to you, you come closer to me. Faithful, powerful, and true—you are my strong Protector! Thank you, Lord. In Jesus's name. Amen.

PERFECT LOVE

There is no fear in love. But perfect love drives out fear, because fear has to do with punishment. The one who fears is not made perfect in love.

1 John 4:18

Lord, I want to live a life full of love, not fear. Will you help me? I know I shouldn't be apprehensive, but I am—maybe because of my past or because I've been hurt by others so often. Help me to experience your love—to receive it, live it, and give it away to others. Love is the best gift ever, and I want to unwrap it in my life. In Jesus's name. Amen.

LEAVING FEAR BEHIND

> In God I trust and am not afraid.
>   What can man do to me?
>
> Psalm 56:11

Lord, I have been walking this well-worn footpath of fear and anxiety for far too long. I want to change course in my thought life and my actions. I want to leave fear behind and set forth on your highway of hope. Lead me to courage as I take this baby step of faith. You are calling; I choose to follow, uncertain, shaking, but willing because I know you are with me. Lead on, Lord, lead on. You are my strong hope. In Jesus's name. Amen.

8

When You're Dealing with Difficult People

Prayers for Grace and Strength

> The righteous person may have many troubles,
> but the LORD delivers him from them all.
>
> Psalm 34:19

My job is great," said Priya. "It's just the people I work with; they drive me crazy!" No matter where you work or with whom you live, there will always be people with different points of view or annoying habits.

Like Priya, maybe you spend most of your day dealing with divas—people who think they are entitled to everything and let everyone else know it. Whether you're frustrated because a driver cut you off in traffic or a family member is on your last nerve, you need strength to cope with difficult people in many areas of life.

It is beyond me how some people can be downright mean. Their words are abusive—even in the workplace. I remember working for a woman who had a flaring temper. She would yell, stomp her high-heeled feet, and throw papers across my desk. I didn't think it was appropriate behavior, so I talked to her about it. She denied everything.

So I went to her superior, a vice president, hoping to get some resolution. He listened to what I had to say and then to my surprise said, "I don't think there's a problem; I think you are the problem." What!? I felt like I was in *The Twilight Zone*. Later, I learned that the woman I worked for and this vice president were having an affair, so he was defending her—even though she was clearly in the wrong. Thankfully, God got me out of that horrible situation when a manager in another department asked me to work for him.

Difficult people can be in our workplaces or, sadly, in our own homes. Maybe you have a relative who's an arrogant know-it-all or an obnoxious drunk. Perhaps your spouse complains constantly or pecks at you like a woodpecker on a tree. Could it be that you have to live with hurtful words and put-downs or someone who is critical and manipulative?

You Have Choices

I'm sure you have your own list of things that bother you as you deal with people who ignore, interrupt, or insult you. No matter what happens or how people treat you, you can choose how you will respond. You can respond defensively and angrily or kindly with respect and tact. You can change the subject. You can walk away. You can choose not to argue and take the high road. You have choices.

Of course, it's natural to be offended when someone hurts your feelings, but what you *do* with that offense—whether you hold it inside and let it fester or release it—makes all the difference. How can you deal with the conflict and strife created by the difficult people in your life?

Jesus had some remarkable things to say about handling conflict and dealing with difficult people, such as loving your enemies (see Matt. 5:44). Human nature often wants to do otherwise. Sometimes the most loving thing to do is to "speak the truth in love" (Eph. 4:15) and say the hard things with kindness and tact but also with boldness and truth.

When someone has hurt you or sinned against you, go to the person who has offended you first. In Matthew 18:15–17, Jesus said, "If your brother or sister sins, go and point out their fault, just between the two of you. If they listen to you, you have won them over. But if they will not listen, take one or two others along, so that 'every matter may be established by the testimony of two or three witnesses.' If they still refuse to listen, tell it to the church; and if they refuse to listen even to the church, treat them as you would a pagan or a tax collector."

What are some other things you can do when dealing with difficult people?

Keep perspective. Hurting people hurt other people. They may have issues in their lives that make them act the way they do. Knowing that may help you better deal with the situation. Often, the problem is not about *you* but about *them*.

Communicate with tact. Don't blame or accuse. Instead, say, "When you [describe their action], I feel [describe how you feel]." For example, "When you interrupt me, I feel like you don't care about what I have to say." Of course, there are times when, despite your best efforts, you may need to leave the room and handle the situation another time so anger can diffuse.

Ask yourself, "What can I learn from this?" Maybe you are learning deeper depths of patience through a challenging relationship or greater dependence on God to help you through tough times.

Pray. Most importantly, pray—for the person who's annoying you and for grace and strength in your response. Ask God how best to handle your challenging situation. God may take you out of it, or he may sustain you while you stay in it. Or knowing the creative God we serve, he may just do something else. Philippians 4:13 states, "I can do all this through him who gives me strength." Know that you cannot handle the situation in your own strength. You may want to get angry and lash out; you may think revenge is the only way, but God can empower you and enable you to reply in God-honoring ways.

Finally, expect things to change. While you cannot change another person, you can alter your own behavior and make different choices with your words and actions.

Coping with difficult people is a part of life. It isn't always easy, but thankfully God is bigger than any obstacle—even that person in your office or your living room. Pray about your challenges, have hope, and watch what happens. God is at work. Be at peace.

A Lesson from a Diamond

Diamonds are like no other gemstone on earth. These precious stones shine with brilliance and glittering beauty. Interestingly, diamonds are formed below the surface of the earth because of very high heat and pressure. When the heat is on in your office because of an annoying co-worker, or a family member is pushing your emotional buttons, remember that something valuable is being formed within you—character, patience, and perseverance. Those traits are worth more than diamonds.

LOVE ANYWAY

Love your enemies and pray for those who persecute you.

Matthew 5:44

Lord, I have a challenging person in my life right now, and sometimes I don't know what to do. You tell us to love our enemies, but my human nature wants to do otherwise. Show me how to love and give me the strength to do so. Pour out your power in me to show kindness, even when it is not merited by another person. Give me discernment to know when to face a situation and when to walk away. I choose the high road of love; protect my heart. In Jesus's name. Amen.

DON'T JUDGE OTHERS

Do not judge, or you too will be judged. For in the same way you judge others, you will be judged, and with the measure you use, it will be measured to you.

Matthew 7:1–2

Lord, sometimes people can be mean, hurtful, or downright obnoxious, and it's hard to understand why. But you know this difficult person. Help me to realize that hurting people hurt other people because they have their own issues to deal with. Maybe this person had a difficult past. It does not excuse the behavior, but it helps me not to be so quick to judge. Please heal my situation with this person. I leave the outcome in your hands. In Jesus's name. Amen.

DEALING WITH GOSSIP AND LIES

We hear that some among you are idle and disruptive. They are not busy; they are busybodies.

2 Thessalonians 3:11

Lord, I can't believe the things other people say, especially when they are hurtful things about me or those I love. Please deal with the gossip and lying that's been going on. Vindicate me, Lord. Defend me and make things right, I pray. Be my advocate for truth. I know that I cannot change others, but I can change how I deal with them. Please give me a right attitude and a new perspective. Please let the truth be known and my honor restored for your glory and your name's sake. In Jesus's name. Amen.

WHEN IT'S HARD TO LOVE OTHERS

Therefore, my dear brothers and sisters, stand firm. Let nothing move you. Always give yourselves fully to the work of the Lord, because you know that your labor in the Lord is not in vain.

1 Corinthians 15:58

Lord, I need help standing firm right now. I feel shaky and uncertain. I want to follow you and do your will, but I have this person in my life who is disruptive. I need your strength to say the right things and to love the way you love. Help me to see beyond the problem to the person who is messing up my life. Give me courage to speak the truth in love, to stand up for myself, and to say the hard things—with kindness but also with boldness and truth. Please make things right. Strengthen me. In Jesus's name. Amen.

A HEART OF PATIENCE

And we urge you, brothers and sisters, warn those who are idle and disruptive, encourage the disheartened, help the weak, be patient with everyone.

1 Thessalonians 5:14

Lord, I need help. Sometimes the last thing I have is patience with this person who annoys me. Help me to be more like you—loving, accepting, and kindhearted. Pour into me your compassionate heart for others. I cannot handle this situation I am in, but you can. Lord, may others see Christ in me. Let me be a person of peace, not of strife or conflict. Use this relationship for your glory, even now, when things are hard. I ask for your help. In Jesus's name. Amen.

THE ROAD TO HOPE

We know that suffering produces perseverance; perseverance, character; and character, hope. And hope does not put us to shame, because God's love has been

90

poured out into our hearts through the Holy Spirit, who has been given to us.

Romans 5:3–5

Lord, it's been a long road with the person who is hard to be around. You know the story, and you know I need help and healing. Please give me strength as I travel this path of perseverance in a tough situation. You are building in me character, and that leads to hope. Along the way I may get weary, but you keep me going. When you pour your love into me, it spills out into the lives of others. May they see Christ in me even when I feel anything but Christlike. Thank you. In Jesus's name. Amen.

GUARDING MY HEART

Above all else, guard your heart,
  for everything you do flows from it.

Proverbs 4:23

Lord, my heart needs protection. I want to be a loving person, an open door. But I also need to know when to close the door of my heart to keep out bad influences or harmful people. Help me to guard my precious heart, my inner life, and have appropriate boundaries. Help me to be wise with how much time I spend with others and what I choose to share. I want to be trusting but also sensible and safe. Protect me, my strong Sentinel. In Jesus's name. Amen.

9

When You Feel Lonely

Prayers for Love and Living Connected

Turn to me and be gracious to me,
for I am lonely and afflicted.

Psalm 25:16

Wayne has a solitary life. Every day he sits behind a computer, alone in a small cubicle at work. At night he sinks into the couch in front of the TV to unwind. He spends much of his free time on the internet—on Facebook or playing games. He has a sense of "virtual community" but not many friends with whom he interacts in person. Because of his lack of social skills, Wayne is often lonely.

Kate is a new mom who's home all day with a newborn. She loves her baby girl, but she misses the companionship and conversation of her colleagues at the office. And Paige, a marketing manager, just moved eight hundred miles across the country to start a new job in a city where she knows no one. She feels a bit lost and disconnected from her friends back home.

There are many reasons why you may feel isolated or alone. Perhaps you've just ended a relationship and friends are scarce, or you're so busy at work that you don't have time to start new friendships—much less maintain the threads of the ones you have already. Maybe you're recovering from an illness or injury, and people are too busy to stop by. Or your self-esteem is so low that you're unwilling or unable to reach out to others to form solid, lasting friendships.

We can feel lonely because we are physically alone or feel left out or alienated even when we are surrounded by people. I remember when I had just moved to a new state and was in the food court at the mall. Dozens of people were around, yet I still felt homesick and alone.

No matter what the reason, it hurts to feel isolated, disconnected, or unnoticed.

I once had a roommate who could not stand to be alone. Lizzie made a point of surrounding herself with people almost constantly, whether it was in person, on the phone, or on the internet. I began to think that her cell phone was permanently glued to her right hand. She abhorred the thought of solitude.

Sometimes we need the peace and quiet that time alone brings; other times we need connection with others. But there's a difference between loneliness and solitude.

Solitude can be replenishing after a hard week at work or in our prayer time with God. With the one who loves us most we can pour out our problems, ask for help, and thank him for all he has done for us. We can also learn to listen. In the stillness, in the quiet, we can hear what God is trying to communicate to us. Away from noise and distractions, we can absorb truth in new ways.

Loneliness is different. One definition says that "loneliness is a painful awareness that we lack close and meaningful contact with others. It involves a feeling of inner emptiness, isolation, and intense longing."[1] You may also feel sad, anxious, or inferior because you are unable to connect with people—or connect with a *certain* person.

The Importance of Connection

We live in a society that exalts self-reliance and where we are more disconnected than ever. The internet has radically changed how we interact with people. On the one hand, it's a fantastic tool. From my living room in Colorado, I can email my dad in Minnesota or Facebook with readers in Brazil. On the other hand, technology may limit a person's face-to-face interactions and close friendships. On Facebook, for instance, we may go *wide* (have a lot of "friends") but not go *deep* (have meaningful relationships with good friends).

We all need to connect with other people. We were created to need each other and to serve each other's needs. Indeed, our longing for love, friendship, and close friends is real. Such things are vital to our emotional well-being. Just as bridges provide a link from one place to another, friendships connect one isolated person to another, and soon community is built.

You can build connections in all areas of life. For example, build:

- *Spiritual community* with people at church or a small group, prayer group, missions team, or one-on-one with someone like-minded
- *Social community* through a bowling league, moms group, singles group, or coffee with friends
- *Intellectual community* with people from work, a book group, or another group with shared interests
- *Physical community* through a sports team, dance class, or workout partner for the gym

- *Neighborhood or city community* through a local playground, a neighborhood block party, or mentoring a disadvantaged youth
- *Virtual community*, but make sure social media connections are not your *only* connections with other people

Connecting with God

Of course, the first person to make a connection with is the most important one. Through prayer and our relationship with God, we have the most primary and meaningful connection possible.

Prayer is talking with God, not at him. It's a holy conversation of both speaking and listening. Your words don't have to be perfect or rehearsed, just real and from your heart. Tell God how you feel and what you need. Thank him for all he has done for you and for those you love. When you don't know what to say, even the simple prayer, "Help!" will reach the loving ears of God.

To overcome loneliness, you may want to start by asking yourself why you feel lonely. Is it because of a recent move or another reason, or have you felt like this for some time? Ask God to make his presence real to you today. Ask him to help you have hope that things can change in your life. You can also ask God to give you courage to reach out to another person or to bring caring relationships— with friends, family, or other new people—into your life. Finally, ask what you can do today to build a bridge to another person.

Jesus said, "And surely I am with you always, to the very end of the age" (Matt. 28:20). When you know God, you are never alone.

A Lesson from an Aspen Grove

On a cool, crisp day in early fall, golden aspen leaves quake in the autumn breeze. As they shimmer, in all their golden beauty, against the backdrop of a clear blue sky, I remember why I love living in Colorado.

Unlike other trees, aspens are connected. While each individual tree stands alone, an aspen grove is literally one organism because its root systems are intertwined.

Likewise, people need community and connection with others in order to thrive. We need bonds and relationships of all kinds—family, friends, community, or people we know from church, sports, or hobby groups. When we choose to intertwine our lives with others, we find emotional fulfillment and a heart to serve others. Even simple acts connect us, like bringing a meal to a friend with a broken arm or calling your grandmother just because. You are not alone. We're all connected.

LORD, HELP MY LONELINESS

Turn to me and be gracious to me,
for I am lonely and afflicted.

Psalm 25:16

Lord, you know the pain I am in right now. I feel so empty and alone. I know I've been isolated and need contact with other people, but sometimes it's hard. Please help me learn how to build bridges to other people. I need closer friendships. I need close-knit community. I long for it. Help me to overcome and find joy again. I ask in Jesus's name. Amen.

NEVER ALONE

And surely I am with you always, to the very end of the age.

Matthew 28:20

Lord, what a comfort it is to know that you are always with me and that you never leave. So many times people disappoint me. I want to trust and make connections with people, but it hasn't happened yet. With you there is peace and stability. You are my strength when I am weak, my true consolation when I am sad. Here in your presence I abide, I dwell. Thank you for always being near. I am never alone. In Jesus's name. Amen.

FIRST LOVE

Jesus replied: "'Love the Lord your God with all your heart and with all your soul and with all your mind.' This is the first and greatest commandment."

Matthew 22:37–38

Lord, I want to thank you for the most important person in my life: you. I choose to put you first and love you. Make your presence real to me today. I need hope that things can change in my life. I don't want to be lonely anymore. I am tired of this longing and ache. Will you give me courage to reach out—or bring caring relationships to me? I want to be more connected with other people, but mostly, Lord, I want to be close to you. I ask in Jesus's name. Amen.

BUILDING COMMUNITY

God sets the lonely in families.

Psalm 68:6

Lord, I need you. I have felt alone and friendless lately. Help me to get connected with my family or people who may become like family to me. Fill this emptiness in me with your love so I can be filled up and have something to offer others. I need community. I need friendship. Please show me where I belong. I want to walk this path of life with others who will build me up, not tear me down. And I want to encourage others, to give and take. I ask in Jesus's name. Amen.

GOD IS FOR ME

What, then, shall we say in response to these things? If God is for us, who can be against us?

Romans 8:31

Lord, it makes me glad to know that you are for me! You, the one who is ultimate love and ultimate authority, designed me and have favor toward me. Thank you. In my desolate, desert times, I have felt so alone, so desperate at times. But when I remember the truth that you are with me and for me, it releases the pain and fills my heart with hope and joy. I am grateful. And I praise your holy name. In Jesus's name. Amen.

I NEED HELP, LORD

The widow who is really in need and left all alone puts her hope in God and continues night and day to pray and to ask God for help.

1 Timothy 5:5

Lord, here I am. I am in a desperate situation. I feel so alone, like I'm in a desert. Please meet me in this desolate place. Every day I pray and ask for help, for relief from the pain in my heart. Help me to hold on to hope, to hold on to you. You are my Wild Hope. You know my needs—emotional, physical, spiritual, and social. You know everything about me. I surrender my needs and ask that you would do what is best. I put my trust in you. I ask in Jesus's name. Amen.

ACCEPTED IN GOD'S FAMILY

I will be a Father to you,
  and you will be my sons and daughters,
    says the Lord Almighty.

2 Corinthians 6:18

Lord, what a privilege it is to be called your son or daughter. Help me to know you as the kind Father you are, the one who loves, accepts, protects, and provides for me. I am humbled by your forgiveness, even when I mess up. Thank you. As your child, teach me how to live with courage and conviction as I seek more connections, relationships, in my life. Help me to find others in the family of God and in my own family with whom I can become closer. Thank you for the gift of your love. In Jesus's name. Amen.

10

When You're Bored

Prayers for Meaning and Purpose

I pray that the eyes of your heart may be enlightened
in order that you may know the hope to which he has
called you.

Ephesians 1:18

If you think being bored is merely having nothing to do, think
again. Although that's one definition, many people find boredom to be a place of inner emptiness and discontent.

Years ago, I worked in a large corporation, and after being
there for twelve years, I was feeling restless. I knew how to do the
work, yet the sameness was tiring. I needed a change. You may
be feeling unfulfilled in your job too. Perhaps it is tedious work,
or it's a job you've been doing for so many years that it no longer
interests you.

I've known times in my life when I've had a full plate of things
to do, but none of them seemed interesting to me. When your life

is full of have-tos, ought-tos, musts, and shoulds instead of things of your own choosing or desire, tedium can set in. Sameness and monotony can make you tired or apathetic. You just don't care anymore, and even if you did, you simply don't have the energy to change. Instead, you yawn and reach for the remote.

Even if you're mostly satisfied with your life, you may have occasional times of boredom—like at a dinner party or on a first date when the person across the table from you drones on and on about something you are simply not interested in. Your mind goes numb. You disengage. Sure, you smile and nod occasionally so it seems like you're listening, but emotionally you've checked out.

Perhaps, like my friends whose kids are grown and gone, your once rambunctious house is now quiet. Or you're retired and still haven't found a way to use the new time on your hands. Whatever the reason you're feeling bored or life-weary, you can discover your passions and purposes again.

If you're feeling lost, it's time to "get found."

Where can we turn to find joy and renew meaning and purpose? Here are some things to consider.

Focus on others. When you feel bored, it could be because most of your time is spent looking inward. When you turn your focus from self to others, something wonderful happens. You find joy again. Serving others brings joy to God's heart, and it can reinvigorate yours.

For example, when Dean was in his early thirties, he faced the daily monotony of working a factory job every day and sitting alone in front of the TV every night. He felt there had to be more to life, but he didn't know what to do. Today, Dean has found renewed meaning in serving others as a volunteer with the Big Brothers Big Sisters program.

Do what energizes you. Mary loves to make jewelry in her spare time. Denise enjoys scrapbooking. And you'll most often find Maria on her bike, usually meandering among the pine trees on a Colorado mountain trail. Doing what you like to do, or trying something new, energizes you.

Start with one thing. Whether you want to change your career or your circumstances, change starts with doing one thing. One small step leads to another, and then another, and you build momentum in your life—a thrust of forward movement.

Start small. Redecorating your living room may seem like a huge task, but you can make a start by rearranging the things you already own. You may want a change of scenery. You could go on a vacation, but you could start by taking a walk. Even if you do the same things every day—like brush your teeth, comb your hair, and get dressed—you can do them in a different order for variety.

Say you want to change your job. Do one thing. Take a book out of the library. Sign up for a class to learn new job skills or call someone who is doing a job similar to what you'd like to do for an "informational interview" (e.g., ask them about the job, what they like and don't like, and what skills you would need to have a similar position). Maybe it's time to reinvent yourself.

Ask, "What is holding me back?" Ask yourself what is keeping you from moving forward in life. Is it a lack of time, money, or other resources? Is it fear or uncertainty about what you really want?

Identify your gifts and abilities. Many books and tests can help you identify your skills or spiritual gifts. Find out where you excel. Knowing and using your gifts and talents are key to finding your purpose in life. And you will find joy as you use them.

Find good company. We all need interaction with people, but if you've found yourself bored lately with the people you've been talking to, you may want to find more interesting people with whom to converse.

Ask God what to do next. If you need direction and motivation, ask God to show you the next step for your life—or for today—to help you get closer to finding joy and meaningful purpose in life.

Why Am I Here?

Finally, but most importantly, true joy comes when you know why you are here. It is the most important thing that will give your life meaning and purpose.

Did you know that God created you to know him and enjoy him? He alone can fill your emptiness with confidence, joy, acceptance, love, and purpose. He is the Author of life, and he has a place for you in his story—complete with your own specific callings, skills, personality, and abilities.

He created you for good purposes. We find purpose in helping others—whether it's serving food to the homeless, working in a food pantry, or simply giving someone a ride to church because she doesn't have a car. Such acts bless others, make us feel good, and give glory to God!

Ephesians 2:10 says that you are God's handiwork; he made you. You are his masterpiece. Let that thought sink in. Even when you don't feel like a priceless work of art, you are. The world tries to mar your original beauty and distort your perception with half-truths and lies, but the truth is that each person is God's work of art—unique and highly valued.

No matter what your role in life, you can be a world changer—with your kids, your co-workers, or your culture. As you identify your gifts and abilities, find what energizes you, do what you love, and know who loves you most, things can change.

God has a purpose for you. He can do all things, and no purpose of his can be thwarted (see Job 42:2).

A Lesson from a Stagnant Pond

Last summer some friends and I stayed at a condo in Keystone, Colorado. From the deck we could see miles of pine-covered mountains and a rapidly flowing river that wound its way beside a scum-covered pond. Cut off from a source of moving water, the pond was stagnant. The rushing river, on the other hand, fed by mountain snowmelt, was fresh and in continual motion. When we are cut off from our source of power, we get sluggish and inactive too. The source, God's Holy Spirit, is life-giving. We need a fresh, constant flow of God's power in our lives, which comes from a connected relationship with him and other believers and from reading and hearing what he has to say in his Word, the Bible. Are you a stagnant pond or a flowing river? Jesus said in John 7:38, "Whoever believes in me, as Scripture has said, rivers of living water will flow from within them."

WHEN I'M FEELING AIMLESS

Many are the plans in a person's heart,
   but it is the LORD's purpose that prevails.

Proverbs 19:21

Lord, sometimes I feel like my life is an empty vacuum. I feel lost, alone, and aimless. Please show me what to do. Fill me with good ideas and a desire to put my heart and hands to tasks that give meaning and purpose. I ask you to direct me. Let your good purposes prevail in my life. You are my true north; show me the right direction. I ask in Jesus's name. Amen.

GOD HAS PLANS AND A PURPOSE FOR ME

The LORD will work out his plans for my life—
   for your faithful love, O LORD, endures forever.

Psalm 138:8 NLT

Lord, I ask that you would help me work through the fears I have about the future. Life is so uncertain. But I can count on you no matter what. Your love is faithful, your guidance is right, and I can trust that you truly have good plans for my life, even when it doesn't feel like it. Despite my feelings, I choose to have faith. Shore up my faith, Lord. I trust you; I thank you. Lead on. In Jesus's name. Amen.

I AM GOD'S WORK OF ART

For we are God's handiwork, created in Christ Jesus to do good works, which God prepared in advance for us to do.

Ephesians 2:10

Lord, sometimes it's hard to imagine myself as a work of art. Sometimes I feel anything but beautiful and worthy. But your Word says that I am your creation, the work of your master craftsmanship. Like a painting or sculpture, you formed and shaped me exactly how I am for a reason. I pray that you would show me the good works you have for me. And empower me with wisdom and strength to do them well for your glory. In Jesus's name. Amen.

SHOW ME THE WAY

Guide me in your truth and teach me,
    for you are God my Savior,
and my hope is in you all day long.

Psalm 25:5

Lord, it makes me glad to know that even on the most boring of days you are at work behind the scenes in my life. Help me to trust you for today and for all my tomorrows. I need to know your truth so I can take steps in the right direction. I need to know more of who you are so my hope is awakened. Help me to break out of this boredom funk and move forward. In Jesus's name. Amen.

WHERE DO I GO FROM HERE?

But now, Lord, what do I look for?
    My hope is in you.

Psalm 39:7

Lord, my life seems to be at a standstill. It's like a stagnant pond. I don't know what to do differently to become a flowing river. I need help to get moving. I've looked to other things to help me break out of this monotony, but their thrill is short-lived. You are my lasting hope; you are the one who can make significant changes in my life. May the power of the Holy Spirit be alive and active in my life. Change me, Lord. I ask for direction. In Jesus's name. Amen.

AMAZING THINGS TO COME

However, as it is written: "What no eye has seen, what no ear has heard, and what no human mind has conceived"—the things God has prepared for those who love him.

1 Corinthians 2:9

Lord, so many times I am tempted to settle for less. I don't always have the energy or the will to hope for changes in my life because things have been so difficult. But you have amazing things prepared for me, and I want to find them, whether they are realized here on earth or in heaven with you. Your promises never fail. Show me all that you have for me and help me not to miss it. I want to have wild hope—hope beyond expectations—in you, the one with the wonder-working power. I ask in Jesus's name. Amen.

WHEN I NEED ENERGY AND STRENGTH

But as for me, I am filled with power,
    with the Spirit of the Lord,
    and with justice and might.

Micah 3:8

Lord, I feel like my get-up-and-go has got-up-and-went. I'm tired and depleted. Nothing seems to interest me anymore. I don't want to live like this, but I don't know how to change. Please fill me with your power so I can get energized and get moving again. Show me one thing I can do today to start to build momentum. I need your help.

I need motivation. Invigorate me, Lord, and help me to find joy and meaningful purpose again. I ask in Jesus's name. Amen.

GOD IS AT WORK IN MY LIFE

For it is God who works in you to will and to act in order to fulfill his good purpose.

Philippians 2:13

Lord, help me to identify what is holding me back in my life and to deal with it. It could be fear, insecurity, or doubt. It could be a lack of finances, time, energy, or know-how. Whatever it is, Lord, I surrender it to you, and I ask for your power and purpose in my life to come forth. You are greater and stronger than any barrier. I choose to trust you. In Jesus's name. Amen.

11

When You've Made Mistakes

Prayers for Forgiveness

> If any of you lacks wisdom, you should ask God, who
> gives generously to all without finding fault, and it
> will be given to you.
>
> James 1:5

Recently, a utility worker in Arizona mistakenly tripped off an electric transmission line and cut power to 1.4 million homes. It was probably enormously embarrassing to the worker because that one small action caused a blackout in San Diego.

Intentionally or unintentionally, we all make mistakes; no one lives error-free. It is part of the human condition. Mistakes will most often cost you something—your time, your money, your reputation, or more. For instance, if you miss one payment on your credit card bill, your rates will go up significantly. Ignore the fine print on a document, and you may wind up with results you never expected. Forget to pick up your child after ballet class, and you've got your hands full of some strong emotions.

While we all make mistakes, it's what we do after a blunder that makes a difference. Whether a mistake was intentional or made out of ignorance—we simply didn't know—we can wallow in regret, run and hide, or choose to learn from the mistake. Sometimes we need forgiveness; other times we need wisdom. Sometimes we need both.

Ask for Forgiveness

Failure can turn to triumph when we ask God for forgiveness, receive it, and learn to discern the ways of wisdom. Certainly, we need wisdom to do things differently and make better choices, but first we need forgiveness.

The mistake you made could have been a small oversight. On the other hand, it could have been willful disobedience, and you need to call it what it is: sin. It's not a popular word today, but a wrongdoing against God is an offense toward him. Sin separates; it disconnects us from God. So in order to be right with God again, to reconnect the relationship, we need forgiveness.

When we are repentant and ask God for forgiveness, he extends it and opens the door to right standing with him again. First John 1:9 says, "If we confess our sins, he is faithful and just and will forgive us our sins and purify us from all unrighteousness."

Even when we mess up, God keeps right on loving us. He is constant and faithful, a loving God but also a God of justice. So when you feel like you're being disciplined, it's for a reason. Because he loves you, he wants things to be made right. After you've asked for forgiveness and he has given it, don't keep beating yourself up emotionally. You may have done something bad, but you are not a bad person. God loves you—always. He may be hurt by your actions at times, but restoration is possible. That's why grace is so amazing. In addition, when God forgives you, it paves the way for you to forgive others.

Even kings can mess up big time. King David lived centuries ago, but he battled many of the same desires people do today. He slept with another man's wife, and there were consequences. Some time later he learned Bathsheba was pregnant. To cover up his sin, David resorted to having her husband, Uriah, killed on the front line of battle. David's sin cost an innocent man his life. You can read this true story in 2 Samuel 11.

Although David tried to cover it up, God knew David's sin and his heart. David repented (see 2 Sam. 12:13), knowing that his punishment could be severe. Instead, he learned a life-changing lesson about God's grace that day. He chronicled his lament and restoration in what is now Psalm 51.

Receive the Gift

When someone gives you a gift, you receive it. That means it passes from their hands to yours; you open the box, take out the item, and use it. And you say thank you. The gift has been given; it also has to be received.

In the same way, God extends the gift of forgiveness when we ask, and we need to receive his gift of forgiveness—to walk in it, to let go of the past, and to move forward. If you have hurt another person by your mistake, you can ask God for the integrity and courage to say you are sorry and to ask him or her for forgiveness.

Then move forward. Don't keep mulling over the mistake in your mind. God forgives and forgets; we need to do the same by forgiving ourselves, walking in the truth, and thanking him for all he has done. It may take some time for your heart to catch up with your head and *feel* forgiven. But whether you feel it or not, the fact remains that God has forgiven you. The feelings will follow.

Remind yourself how loving and gracious God is; he does not treat us as our sins or mistakes deserve. He treats us infinitely better. Read Psalm 103:8–12 for a good reminder about God's compassionate heart.

Wisdom: Learn to Discern

When we make mistakes, we want to know what to do differently next time. As you take the time to talk with God one-on-one in prayer, ask him for wisdom. Read the books of wisdom in the Bible; two of them are Psalms and Proverbs. "A house is built by wisdom and becomes strong through good sense. Through knowledge its rooms are filled with all sorts of precious riches and valuables," says Proverbs 24:3–4 (NLT).

Discernment is good judgment. It's knowing right from wrong. It is also having the spiritual sensitivity to know what is truth and what's a lie, when to act or when to wait, when to speak or when to be silent. Discernment comes as wisdom is developed in your life. Wisdom develops as you follow the Leader. Are you trusting God's leadership, listening to what he has to say, and acting on it? Is he the one you run to first for advice? Is he the head of your household?

Oftentimes, as we gain wisdom, we also unlearn foolishness. We may have made mistakes in the past because we were following worldly ways instead of God's wisdom. What we read, hear, and see shapes us. Media and popular culture often try to sell us a bill of goods that says one thing when the Bible teaches another.

For example, the world says it's okay to have sex before marriage, while God values purity. It's not that God is a prude. He loves you so much that he wants the very best for you. He wants to spare you the pain of a heart-wrenching breakup when you've been too involved physically. In addition, the physical act of love between a man and a woman that God created for marriage is special and sacred; there is so much more meaning to it than can be found in a one-night stand or sex as recreation outside of a marriage commitment. God's ways are different from the world's ways, but his ways are always based on the highest love for you.

Prayer Changes Things

Never underestimate the power of prayer. Nothing you have done or can do will keep you out of reach of the ears of our loving Lord. God can do anything; we simply need to ask in faith. "Prayer," says Steven Furtick, "is the arena where our faith meets God's abilities."[1]

In this life, you and I will make mistakes. God is not looking for perfection. He knows your heart and cares more about your intentions. When you ask, God will give you strength to live in the present and not keep looking over your shoulder at the past. He will guide and empower you to make wiser choices and live in freedom and peace.

A Lesson from the Earth's Perfect Orbit

The planet we live on is immense. I don't know what scientists used for a scale, but they say the earth is 8,000 miles in diameter and weighs roughly 6.6×10^{21} tons.[2] It is 93 million miles from the sun and rotates on its axis, turning and spinning as we live, work, and play. One of the most remarkable ways God reveals his wisdom is through the earth's perfect orbit—too close to the sun and we'd fry; too far away and we'd freeze. Either way, the results would extinguish life. Thankfully, God doesn't make mistakes. Instead, we are exactly where we're supposed to be in our place in space. Ask God to keep you in the center of his will, in your own personal orbit around the one who is wise, kind, loving, and just.

FORGIVE ME, LORD

If we confess our sins, he is faithful and just and will forgive us our sins and purify us from all unrighteousness.

1 John 1:9

Lord, I have messed up. I have sinned against you and others in making this mistake. What a mess. I was wrong, and I am sorry. Thank you for your faithfulness and that you never turn your back on me. I ask for your forgiveness. Help me to receive it, to walk in it, and to move forward. Heal me, Lord. I ask in Jesus's name. Amen.

NO CONDEMNATION

Therefore, there is now no condemnation for those who are in Christ Jesus.

Romans 8:1

Lord, it often seems that people want to shame, blame, and criticize when I have done something wrong, but your Word tells me that in Christ there is no condemnation. Because of the price you paid with your life, I am forgiven and set free. How can I thank you for such an indescribable gift? That you remember my sin no more and choose to show mercy is freeing. Thank you. I receive your gift of grace, and I ask for the power to live more wisely. I ask in Jesus's name. Amen.

GOD GIVES WISDOM

For the LORD gives wisdom;
from his mouth come knowledge and understanding.

Proverbs 2:6

Lord, I am humbled and grateful for the wisdom you display. Your knowledge and understanding greatly surpass those of the wisest person on earth. They are more than I can comprehend. When I don't know, you have the answer. When I am uncertain, you are sure. You know the end from the beginning in all matters. You see the bigger picture and what I cannot. May your name be praised for all that you are and all that you do! In Jesus's name. Amen.

CLEANSE MY HEART

Teach me your way, LORD,
    that I may rely on your faithfulness;
give me an undivided heart,
    that I may fear your name.

Psalm 86:11

Lord, life can be such a struggle at times. I want to do the right thing, but I mess up. I want to follow your way, but things in the world call out to me. I feel conflicted inside. Give me an undivided heart and draw me nearer to you. I need to know your ways, and I need the empowerment to be faithful and obedient to all you call me to. I give you my whole heart. Cleanse me from sin and make me right with you. I am relying on you for wisdom and healing. In Jesus's name. Amen.

SHOW ME YOUR TRUTH, LORD

See to it that no one takes you captive through hollow and deceptive philosophy, which depends on human tradition and the elemental spiritual forces of this world rather than on Christ.

Colossians 2:8

Lord, I live in a world that is so polarized. It can be confusing when I am pulled in two different directions of thought—human tradition and God's way. I don't want to be deceived by things that seem right but go against everything you stand for. Show me your truth and righteousness in ways that I can understand and apply to my life. I choose you. I choose life. Move me forward with wisdom and strength to make right choices. For your glory and your name's sake. In Jesus's name. Amen.

THE WORTH OF WISDOM: PRICELESS

Blessed are those who find wisdom,
  those who gain understanding,
for she is more profitable than silver
  and yields better returns than gold.

Proverbs 3:13–14

Lord, when it's all said and done, I want to be a person of wisdom, not folly. I desire deeper understanding of your truth in every area of my life. Like one who hunts for buried treasure, I seek the nuggets of truth you have for me. Thank you for the gift of wisdom, which is better than silver or gold or anything money can buy. Your insight, your knowledge, your understanding? Priceless. Thank you for all you give to me. In Jesus's name. Amen.

12

When You've Been Mistreated

Prayers for Justice

For I, the Lord, love justice;
I hate robbery and wrongdoing.

Isaiah 61:8

If you've ever had your home or car broken into, you know how violating such an act can feel. It's happened to me twice. Break-ins to your vehicle are one thing; break-ins to your inner life can be devastating. Perhaps you've known the sting of rejection or betrayal from a friend or your spouse. Whether it's a slap across the face or a slap across the heart, abuse of any kind is hurtful—and simply wrong.

We are a scarred people. Although you don't see the inner cuts and bruises caused by cruel words or actions, they are there. In your humanness, you may feel like harboring resentment or feelings of revenge. You've been hurt, and you want payback. But those feelings of animosity are like misguided ships that try to dock in the harbor of your heart. Don't let them.

We all handle pain differently. But emotional pain doesn't have to stay inside festering. Restoration can come. Brokenness can be restored.

When you open your heart to forgiveness and, by the power of God, choose to release the ones who have harmed you, there is no longer room for offense. Instead, you begin to feel something you haven't felt in a long time: peace, joy, and inner strength.

Justice Is Served

One of the biggest reasons people don't want to forgive someone who's hurt them is because they mistakenly believe that the person will get away with his or her crime against them. *If I forgive them*, you may think, *then they will be off the hook or they will think I condone their behavior.* You think they should suffer—and do so at your hands. Instead, when you forgive, you are releasing the other person from your hands and giving them to God to handle; *he* will ensure justice is served.

Release the Pain

When you don't forgive, the pain is like acid; it begins to eat away at your heart. You lose your joy, you turn inward, or you become a hardened and angry person. Ask yourself, *What am I holding on to so tightly? What do I need to let go of?*

God has first forgiven us and asks us to forgive others. Jesus said, "For if you forgive other people when they sin against you, your heavenly Father will also forgive you. But if you do not forgive others their sins, your Father will not forgive your sins" (Matt. 6:14–15).

Forgiving someone who has wronged you is for *you*. Whether or not he says he is sorry, whether or not he asks for forgiveness, forgive in your heart. It may sound difficult, but with the power of God, we can do what we never thought we had the courage to do.

Receive Freedom

Forgiveness releases the pain and frees you. No longer handcuffed to misery, you find bitterness receding and joyfulness returning. That person no longer has control of your life or emotions. Instead of a victim, you are a victorious person who has overcome.

Forgiveness doesn't necessarily mean you have to reconcile or spend time with people who have hurt you. Sometimes the wisest and healthiest thing to do is to stay away from them and have boundaries to protect your heart from further pain.

A fresh wind is blowing. It's the freedom you feel when you've forgiven those who have mistreated you. Will you choose to harbor bitterness and resentment, or will you find liberty—in forgiving others because you have been forgiven first by God? Newfound joy and lasting peace are possible. The choice is yours.

A Lesson from a Mountain Switchback

If you're driving or hiking in the Rocky Mountains, you're sure to find winding roads in zigzag patterns called switchbacks. Like a mountain switchback, the path toward forgiveness isn't always straight or smooth. It can be treacherous terrain, littered with bitterness and complicated by emotions that twist and wind in unpredictable ways around the landscape of your heart. Forgiving someone who has wronged you is a journey—from hurt and anger to freedom and peace. But you don't have to walk alone. With Christ as your guide and strong defense, you can do what you never thought possible—release resentment and forgive someone who's wronged you. Hold on to the wild hope of Christ. He knows the way.

FORGIVING OTHERS

For if you forgive other people when they sin against you, your heavenly Father will also forgive you. But if you do not forgive others their sins, your Father will not forgive your sins.

Matthew 6:14–15

Lord, sometimes it is hard to wrap my head around the concept of forgiveness. It seems impossible in my human strength. But your Word says that with you everything is possible. Even this. So I begin by asking you to forgive me first; show me if I have done anything wrong in this situation. Help me to be right with you. I receive your forgiveness. And I ask you to help me extend that same mercy to this person who has wronged me. Help me to forgive—and live again. In Jesus's name. Amen.

DON'T RETALIATE; GOD WILL AVENGE

Do not take revenge, my dear friends, but leave room for God's wrath, for it is written: "It is mine to avenge; I will repay," says the Lord.

Romans 12:19

Lord, when people wrong me, I often feel like they owe me. I want repayment; more so, I want justice. And yet you tell me I need to release my offenders to you, the just Judge, and take my hands off. I am learning that they are not off the hook for their wrongdoings but are now on your hook for justice. You avenge. As much as I want to hold on, I choose to release my offenders to you. Help me to let go, knowing you will take care of the situation. I trust you. In Jesus's name. Amen.

LOVE JUSTICE; HATE WRONGDOING

For I, the LORD, love justice;
    I hate robbery and wrongdoing.
In my faithfulness I will reward my people
    and make an everlasting covenant with them.

Isaiah 61:8

Lord, I don't know where I would be without you. I am so glad that you are a God of love and justice. You hate when your children are wronged. It grieves your heart. What a blessing it is to know that you are faithful and that you come through for me as my Advocate, my strong Support, my Hero. Instead of a victim, I am an overcoming, victorious person because of you! Thank you. I praise you. In Jesus's name. Amen.

DEALING WITH ANGER

"In your anger do not sin": Do not let the sun go down while you are still angry.

Ephesians 4:26

Lord, I need help. I am so angry about my situation right now. I don't know what to do. I am so glad that you know all the details. You know everything about my life, and you have the power to heal and change things for the better. Thank you that I have a right to be angry for what's been done to me. Help me not to sin in the midst of it. I choose to release the fury inside of me; here, take this pain. Heal my heart, my past, my memories—all my scars inside and out. I ask for freedom and peace. In Jesus's name. Amen.

LOVE AND JUSTICE

Righteousness and justice are the foundation of your
    throne;
    love and faithfulness go before you.

Psalm 89:14

Lord, so many people seem to have misplaced their sense of right and wrong. They can be dishonest or downright mean. The very basis of who you are is integrity—you make promises and keep them. You value acceptance and kindness; your heart is filled with compassion toward all. Where would I be without your justice? Thank you, my faithful God, for restoration. My strength. My loving God. In Jesus's name. Amen.

JUSTICE WILL COME

Yet the LORD longs to be gracious to you;
    therefore he will rise up to show you compassion.
For the LORD is a God of justice.
    Blessed are all who wait for him!

Isaiah 30:18

Lord, you have seen me through this hard time. You know all I have been through, and I thank you that we are on a heart-healing journey. Empower me to forgive, to release the pain, and to receive the peace and freedom waiting on the other side of surrender. You are a God of justice, and I trust that one day all things will be made right. I choose to wait as you heal and help me. Thank you for your compassion and grace to me. You are amazing. In Jesus's name. Amen.

13

When You Can't Break a Bad Habit or Addiction

Prayers for Overcoming

Jesus looked at them and said, "With man this is impossible, but with God all things are possible."

Matthew 19:26

Sam has a problem with alcohol. He goes to church and loves God, but he's racked up two DUIs in the past five years. Alexa, a recent college grad, has struggled with anorexia since she was a teenager. Her controlling parents and their towering expectations left her feeling that food was the only thing she could control in her life. She can't seem to stop or change her unhealthy behavior.

Even good people have bad habits—or life-altering addictions.

In fact, millions of us have cravings we want to beat, but they seem to have a vicelike grip on our appetites and actions. Overeating (or other food-related issues), smoking, gambling, and overspending are some of the most common struggles. Others battle sex addiction, pornography, or addiction to the computer. They are obsessed—and stuck.

Poor diet and lack of exercise are bad habits Darcy faces nearly every day. She loves fast food, and when a stressful day brings on cravings and the need for comfort—which is often—she finds it easiest to swing through a nearby drive-through restaurant and order whatever she likes. It's fast, it's easy, and the food tastes good. Darcy knows that her fat- and calorie-laden fast-food habit, combined with her desk job and sedentary life, are a dangerous combination for her health. She wants to make better choices, but sometimes she simply doesn't care.

Whether your craving is for drugs or donuts, whether you struggle with an addiction or a bad habit, you'll need more than willpower—or won't power—to overcome and find freedom. Is there a way to break free from whatever is keeping you stuck? It's not always easy, but by the power of God, it is possible.

Defining Habit and Addiction

What's the difference between a bad habit and an addiction? You may have a pattern of unhealthy behavior or a routine that bothers you or those around you, and some call that a bad habit. You're always running late, and it annoys your friends. You bite your fingernails when you're nervous. Or you have a problem with swearing, and you want to stop once and for all.

The word *addiction* describes "a recurring compulsion by an individual to engage in some specific activity, despite harmful consequences, as deemed by the user themselves to their individual health, mental state, or social life."[1] Another definition for substance abuse states that addiction is when "dependence is at such a point that stopping is very difficult and causes severe physical and mental reactions from withdrawal."[2]

The effects from an addiction can be wearing and potentially lethal, from a hangover to lingering health problems, like liver or lung disease. Continual harmful choices wear away at you physically, emotionally, and spiritually. I've seen them break up families, destroy relationships, and put fully functional people into physical or emotional prisons.

Why are we so bent on destroying ourselves?

Excuses, Excuses

The reasons we choose bad habits or harmful addictions are many, but the main ones are to alleviate pain or produce pleasure. You're depressed, bored, or feeling huge amounts of peer pressure. You didn't plan on getting addicted; you thought you could stop your behavior at any time. Maybe you're thinking right now, *It's not that big of a deal. I'm only human. Everyone does it.* On the other hand, you may sincerely want to do the right thing, but then your cravings take over. You feel stuck in this pattern.

Sadly, it's nothing new. The apostle Paul struggled with doing the right thing centuries ago. He made this lament in the book of Romans (the comments in italic are mine):

For I do not do the good I want to do, but the evil I do not want to do—this I keep on doing. (7:19)

I've felt like that at times.

Now if I do what I do not want to do, it is no longer I who do it, but it is sin living in me that does it. (7:20)

Sin is trying to master me and take over. That explains a lot.

What a wretched man I am! Who will rescue me from this body that is subject to death? (7:24)

I don't want to be like this anymore! I need help.

Thanks be to God, who delivers me through Jesus Christ our Lord! (7:25)

Help me to overcome, Lord. Thank you for your power to do what I cannot.

Heart Holes

Many times addictions or bad habits are attempts to fill up the holes in our hearts, the empty spaces where love and acceptance should be but for whatever reason are not. We try to fill these gaping holes with massive amounts of food, way too much alcohol, or our comfort item of choice. But we are never satiated; the inner emptiness remains.

We have real needs that must be met. We need to eat in order to live; we need love, peace, comfort, and rest. But when we strive to meet legitimate needs in unhealthy and sometimes harmful ways, they can turn into sin; they are desires gone wild. When we are tempted to take the good things God created *beyond* the boundary of God's will:

- Physical rest becomes laziness
- Enjoyment of food becomes gluttony
- An ability to profit becomes greed
- Communication becomes gossip
- Conscientiousness becomes perfectionism
- Carefulness becomes fear[3]

Stopping a bad habit or an addiction may seem impossible. You may have been doing something for so long that it's a part of you. But you can overcome and find victory in this extremely challenging area of life. Breaking free from the chains that bind you happens through the healing power of God.

Breaking Free

Stopping an addiction—even a bad habit—can be extremely difficult because something wants to master us or control our lives. Who or what is your master? Whom will you follow? In 1 Corinthians 6:12, the apostle Paul says, "Not everything is beneficial. 'I have the right to do anything'—but I will not be mastered by anything." Oftentimes, we need to address the deception that says, "*This* will make me happy; this alone will fulfill all my needs."

There is a battle raging within each of us—an internal battle between the flesh and the Spirit, God's Holy Spirit. We make choices to satisfy either the body (our flesh), which lead to misery, or the Spirit—choices that lead to life and the fruit of the Spirit (love, joy, peace, patience, kindness, goodness, etc.). It comes down to this: Will you choose to focus on the Spirit or your human desires? The fact is, we can't beat addictions simply by gritting our teeth and trying harder. We need God's power in us to give us the strength to overcome. When we cannot, God can!

Freedom from making unhealthy choices comes as we pray—and take action. Ask God to deliver you from your habit or addiction. Ask others to pray with and for you—you need reinforcements! "Watch and pray so that you will not fall into temptation. The spirit is willing, but the flesh is weak" (Matt. 26:41). Ask God for strength and courage.

My great-aunt Cile overcame her fifty-year smoking habit through prayer. She said it was a true testament to God's power because she had tried to quit unsuccessfully for years. Cile had been a heavy cigarette smoker most of her adult life, and as her eightieth birthday approached, she was diagnosed with emphysema. For months she asked God to deliver her from her tobacco addiction, especially with her new diagnosis. When God finally delivered her, Cile was ecstatic; she knew she could not have done it on her own. Once clean, she saved up her cigarette money each month and used the cash to buy something special for herself or treat her great-nieces to lunch to celebrate her victory.

We need to believe that God has the power and the willingness to work in *our* lives too, not just in other people's messes. Psalm 77:14 says, "You are the God who performs miracles; you display your power among the peoples."

It may be time to evict the messages in your brain that say it will never happen, you can't overcome, or that victory is for other people. That's where renewing your mind comes in—replacing the lies with God's timeless truths. "Do not conform to the pattern of this world, but be transformed by the renewing of your mind. Then you will be able to test and approve what God's will is—his good, pleasing and perfect will" (Rom. 12:2).

When Jesus Christ lives in us, he empowers us to stop, pray, and choose wisely instead of acting based on our feelings. Flee temptation, walk away from the bottle or the brownies. It may be hard; it may be frustrating. You may take three steps forward then two steps back, but you are making progress. You can live in the unchanging promises of God to heal and help you.

God can also use other people to help heal our bad habits and addictions, such as a Christian counselor who has been trained in the area of addictions. Don't be afraid to seek wise counsel when you need it.

What Will You Choose?

Right now you are at a crossroads. You stand before two paths. One says, "Follow your addiction or bad habit," and the other says, "Follow me. I will help you overcome."

As you make one right choice, then another, a series of continual right choices leads to a breakthrough and beyond. When you ask, the power of the Holy Spirit does what you can never do: walks with you through the healing process, breaks the heavy chains that hold you captive, and gives you the strength to say no to unhealthy things and yes to life.

Freedom is calling. How will you reply?

A Lesson from the Mountain Pine Beetle

In the past decade, an insect issue in the American West has created a growing danger for forest fires. Acres of green pine forests in Colorado and other states are now a rusty-red landscape of dead trees because of a voracious infestation of the Mountain Pine Beetle. To date, these insects have killed off an estimated 3.9 million acres of lodgepole pine across the Rocky Mountains, and forests have burned. It's amazing how such small bugs can cause such a large amount of devastation. In the same way, our bad habits or addictions can start with a few small choices and spread, causing untold destruction in our own lives and in the lives of those around us. Positive or negative, what we do affects others.

RENEWING MY MIND

Do not conform to the pattern of this world, but be transformed by the renewing of your mind. Then you will be able to test and approve what God's will is—his good, pleasing and perfect will.

Romans 12:2

Lord, I have been rebelling for a long time. I want to change. I don't want to battle this thing any longer. Please transform me and my bad habits. I may not do this perfectly, but I'm starting by surrendering my addiction to you. Help me to be aware of what I'm feeding my mind, my thought life. Empower me with your might to stand strong on this new path. I ask in Jesus's mighty name. Amen.

STRENGTH FOR WEAKNESS

Watch and pray so that you will not fall into temptation. The spirit is willing, but the flesh is weak.

Matthew 26:41

Lord, I need your strength. I want to do the right thing, but I'm so weak sometimes. I say that I want to change, and then I'm back doing what I don't want to do! It can be so frustrating. So now I pray against these temptations, believing that you have the might to withstand any force—even this habit that's been in my life for so long. Help me. I ask in Jesus's name. Amen.

HELP ME OVERCOME

It is for freedom that Christ has set us free. Stand firm, then, and do not let yourselves be burdened again by a yoke of slavery.

Galatians 5:1

Lord, I have been stuck in this habit like a prison. Come and free me! I want to live right, to live clean. It's such a struggle sometimes. But you know my heart is toward you, even when I fail. I don't want to be a slave to my cravings. Liberate me, open the prison door, and let me walk in freedom and peace. There is more to this life, and I want to find it and use my life to serve others and give you glory. I am relying totally on you. I ask in Jesus's name. Amen.

GOD'S POWER

You are the God who performs miracles;
  you display your power among the peoples.

Psalm 77:14

Lord, I remember the miracles you did in the past. You parted the Red Sea so people could walk across on dry land. You healed the blind and made the lame walk. You can do anything! I need you to do a wonder in my life. And I am believing for healing and freedom. Break the chains that bind me as you have done before for others. Deliver me. Thank you. I praise you. In Jesus's holy name. Amen.

I CAN'T DO IT ON MY OWN

Are you so foolish? After beginning by means of the Spirit, are you now trying to finish by means of the flesh?

Galatians 3:3

Lord, I have tried and failed so many times to beat this habit. Finally, I am learning that I can't do it in my own human effort. I need the Holy Spirit's power to change. Forgive me for making foolish choices. Forgive me for being self-centered and making people or things I crave into an idol when I should be worshiping you, Lord. I am sorry. I need you and ask for help and hope for better days. In Jesus's name. Amen.

THANK YOU FOR DELIVERANCE

Thanks be to God, who delivers me through Jesus Christ our Lord!

Romans 7:25

Lord, I'm learning that there will always be struggles in life, but I overcome through Jesus. You deliver me! Thank you for dying on the cross for me. You shed your blood to pay the price for my awful sins—and the sins of the entire world. You died and rose again, victorious, so we can be overcomers. I am truly thankful. Your strength gives me real hope for lasting changes in my life. In Jesus's name. Amen.

14

When You're Dealing with Grief and Loss

Prayers for Comfort and Hope

Hear my prayer, LORD,
listen to my cry for help;
do not be deaf to my weeping.

Psalm 39:12

Loss and tragedy are twin heartaches Julia knows all too well. A strong, competent woman, Julia is the kind of highly focused person who works hard at her career and has a beautiful, well-functioning home. Her "keep on task" motto is coupled with a generous, encouraging heart. But this caring and capable woman has been stretched in ways she never could have fathomed.

A few years ago, Julia lost her mother and young daughter and broke her pelvis in a tragic car accident. Her husband lost control of the car and drove into a tree when he experienced a brain seizure. Sadly, Julia was unable to attend her daughter's funeral because she was in the hospital recovering from her injuries. But one note of goodness in the midst of pain was that the day before the accident her little girl had prayed to receive Jesus Christ into her heart at vacation Bible school.

Julia and her husband both survived the physical trauma, but the emotional fallout has lasted for years. Today, Julia is still recovering from the awful day that changed her life forever. She still goes to counseling and often has trouble sleeping. While the pain of her losses may never go away totally, it has lessened with time. Now, her focus is forward. Every day she gets up, gets dressed, and seeks to brighten the day for others. Hope is reawakening, like the first fragile crocuses bursting from snowy ground in springtime.

Loss touches our lives in many ways, whether it's through divorce, death, or the death of a dream. A woman learns she can never bear children. A business owner discovers his partner has deceived him, and now he's financially wiped out. Foreclosure on your dream home, financial setbacks, or a disabling illness or injury can be life-shattering. Disaster changes the landscape of your life. You stand amid the rubble and the wreckage, and you wonder how you will ever cope with such loss.

Nehemiah's Story

Bouncing back from tragedy takes time—a lot of time. It also takes comfort, support, and an abundance of prayer.

Nehemiah found help and hope in the rubble of ruin. Though he lived centuries ago, his life lessons still apply to us today. A Jewish man in a foreign land, Nehemiah worked for the king of Persia. When he heard news that the city of Jerusalem lay in ruins and its walls had been burned and broken, Nehemiah was greatly distressed and saddened. His heart broke for his people. In ancient times, city walls were essential for security and protection against the danger of all kinds of enemies.

Nehemiah prayed to God for the right words to say to his boss, a very powerful king. He prayed and fasted and prayed again. He praised God, asked for forgiveness, and presented his request to the king.

The humble servant found favor. The king not only gave Nehemiah his permission but also gave him a guarantee of safe passage with special papers and officers to accompany him. Plus, he received permission to get timber from the royal park, supplies to be used for beams. It took courage to ask. It took even more courage to make the long, arduous journey and rebuild the city walls. But Nehemiah was confident God was with him.

Once in Jerusalem, Nehemiah enlisted help. Most of the volunteer workers were not skilled as wall builders, but they set about rebuilding and worked heartily. Then, worn out and frustrated, the builders began to focus more on the rubble around them than on the progress they had made. Nehemiah 4:10 reads, "Meanwhile, the people in Judah said, 'The strength of the laborers is giving out, and *there is so much rubble* that we cannot rebuild the wall' " (emphasis added).

Have you ever felt like that? Like everything is crumbling around you and the pieces of your problems lay at your feet like the wreckage from a collapsed building. It's too much. You can't do this. You are simply overwhelmed.

Nehemiah was constantly in prayer. He and his volunteer wall builders regrouped, working hard for a cause they believed in. When opposition came from officials, they prayed—and posted guards to keep themselves safe. When news of impending enemy attacks came, they prayed—and guarded the city as they kept on working.

Finally, the wall was rebuilt and the city repopulated. The people praised God for all he had done for them. After all that had transpired, they celebrated, as Nehemiah said to the people, "Go and enjoy choice food and sweet drinks, and send some to those who have nothing prepared. This day is holy to our Lord. Do not grieve, for the joy of the LORD is your strength" (Neh. 8:10).

Rebuilding from Loss

God is all about redeeming loss and pain and healing wounds of all kinds. He is the Master at rebuilding, whether it's rubble in the streets of Jerusalem or the wreckage in your heart.

We may try to deal with tragedy and the ensuing emotions that follow—sadness, anger, resentment, or guilt—in unhealthy ways. Sometimes we don't know what to do, so we do nothing and hope that one day the pain will simply go away. Navigating the strange and stormy waters of grief is hard. But not impossible. Everyone's healing journey is different. Yours may take longer than mine. God may use different methods to lead you from sorrow to joy. And that's okay. He is God. He knows what he is doing. We simply need to trust him.

How do you find your way forward through the grieving process? No matter what type of loss you have incurred, comfort and support are the first steps. They can come from the warm embrace of a close friend, a listening ear, or kind words. We need our friends to help us remember what we already know or to say nothing and simply be there with us in the midst of the pain.

Many people find soul support as they journal, writing down their prayers or their feelings. Healing also comes through rest or a change of scenery. The beauty of nature, God's creation, is restorative.

Knowing God is with you and that he is your Comforter brings peace, as the words of Matthew 5:4 affirm: "Blessed are those who mourn, for they will be comforted." Healing also comes as you release your anguish through your tears. Cling to God's promises, hold on to hope, and surrender your pain to him in prayer.

Instead of holding your feelings inside, it can be helpful to talk about what happened with caring friends, family members, or a Christian counselor who can help you process the pain. Grief unprocessed, ignored, or denied festers. Processing the pain brings release and relief.

Worship and the Word

When you are feeling hopeless, the most powerful thing you can do is worship. Despair cannot journey where praise and worship reside. You may be too grief-stricken to know what to say. But you can put on a worship music CD or just sit with your eyes closed and ask God to heal your heart as you rest and focus on his amazing love and gentle comfort.

As we give God our praises, he gives us his presence. Focusing on his character and what he has done for us lifts us to a new place. God is great, and he is worthy of our praises. Like rain soaks the desert and brings forth cactus blossoms, worship and prayer bring renewal to a withering heart.

Spending time reading God's Word also brings comfort and hope. Now is the time to discover more of the treasure that is the Word of God. It's your spiritual food, nourishment every day but essential in times of need. "For everything that was written in the past was written to teach us, so that through the endurance taught in the Scriptures and the encouragement they provide we might have hope" (Rom. 15:4). Open the Bible; there's hope inside. The other side of pain is joy; the other side of darkness is light. There is life after loss.

In March 2011, a tsunami caused by an 8.9 magnitude earthquake devastated northeastern Japan. It caused widespread destruction and extensive damage to coastal cities. The official death toll exceeded nine thousand. The landscape is now a sea of debris; a once-thriving community is a veritable wasteland.

Recently, I watched a TV program about the disaster, and one survivor said, "There's a different kind of strength you find after you've survived something terrible." Tragedies can undo us; they can also make us stronger.

Life may be challenging for you right now; you may wonder how things will ever change. Take heart. Even in your darkest times, the hope of Christ shines brighter. When you are weak, he is your strong comfort. When you are exhausted, he is your strength—firm and secure. The Light of the World shines as your beacon—a lighthouse in the midst of the storm to guide you to safe harbor.

Light always overcomes the darkness.

A Lesson from a Redwood Tree

The redwood trees in California have a secret. These centuries-old giants—three hundred feet or taller—have a unique ability to withstand fire. In addition to their high branches and the dense bark that provides protection, redwood trees lack a flammable resin on their bark (which most other types of trees have), rendering them almost fireproof. Even if the heat of a forest fire becomes so intense it does burn the tree, the roots often survive because they are buried in the cool, moist soil. And in time, new sprouts begin to appear. Triumph after tragedy.

You may have suffered unspeakable losses; you may feel as if your life will never be the same. But as with the redwoods, new life—a different life—can sprout again. As you get back to the roots of truth in your life, regrowth comes. The heart is surprisingly resilient. Remember, you are God's child. He is with you always. God loves you with an everlasting love. He is your comfort, and he will work out all things for good. Trust God for new hope—and healing.

HEAR MY CRY, LORD

Hear my prayer, LORD,
    listen to my cry for help;
do not be deaf to my weeping.

Psalm 39:12

Lord, I come before you sad today. You know my heart; you see my tears and hear my cries for help in this time of adversity. I cannot believe this has happened. Some days I am just numb. But you are with me, and that makes all the difference. I am not alone. Help me through this time of trouble, Lord. I know you are stronger than anything that comes against me, and I put my trust in you. I'm leaning on you, Lord. In Jesus's name I pray. Amen.

WHEN I NEED COMFORT

Praise be to . . . the God of all comfort, who comforts us in
all our troubles, so that we can comfort those in any trouble
with the comfort we ourselves receive from God.

2 Corinthians 1:3–4

Lord, I need you. I need a holy hug to comfort my grief-weary heart. Let me rest in the comfort of your presence—a place of love, acceptance, and peace. Though the storm of pain rages on, captain my journey back to joy. With all of the consolation and reassurance I receive from you may I one day comfort others in their time of need. In Jesus's name. Amen.

HEAL MY BROKEN HEART

He heals the brokenhearted
    and binds up their wounds.

Psalm 147:3

Lord, I am completely heartbroken. My heart feels like it's been shattered into thousands of tiny pieces, like glass on a hardwood floor. How could this happen? Please heal my wounded heart and make something beautiful and worthy from this mess. Rebuild me, Lord. As you take the pieces of the past and form them into the mosaic of my life, help me to trust you. May I give you all the praise for all you are making me to be, for healing me, and for making me whole again. In Jesus's name. Amen.

THE LORD IS WITH ME

Even though I walk
    through the darkest valley,
I will fear no evil,
    for you are with me;
your rod and your staff,
    they comfort me.

Psalm 23:4

Lord, I have been through some dark valleys lately. The shadows are scary, and depression seems like it will overtake me. But you tell me that you are with me and I don't need to fear. Your protection surrounds me, your comfort soothes me. You provide strong assurance that even though today seems dark I have the Light of the World, Jesus Christ, on whom I can rely. I cling to you. In Jesus's name. Amen.

SOWING TEARS, REAPING JOY

Those who sow with tears
    will reap with songs of joy.
Those who go out weeping,
    carrying seed to sow,
will return with songs of joy,
    carrying sheaves with them.

Psalm 126:5–6

Lord, I give you my tears of grief and sorrow. As they fall to the ground, help me to remember that this pain is not for nothing. One day I will have joy again! Like the farmer who plants seeds and harvests armloads of wheat, may I reap a harvest of blessings, joyfulness, and peace. Grow in me strength and courage as I wait on you. Help me to find joy in each day, grateful for all you have done for me in the past and all you are doing in my life. I am yours. In Jesus's name. Amen.

GOD'S WORD GIVES HOPE

For everything that was written in the past was written to teach us, so that through the endurance taught in the Scriptures and the encouragement they provide we might have hope.

Romans 15:4

Lord, thank you for the Word of God in my own language so I can read for myself what you have to say. Your words teach me new things. They open my eyes to bright hope and give me strength to carry on when I am weak and worn. In the Bible, I find courage when I am afraid. Your words have power because you have power—and you delight to help your children. As I read your words and look to you, please heal my heart and help me to find my way forward. In Jesus's name. Amen.

JOY WILL COME AGAIN

He will yet fill your mouth with laughter
and your lips with shouts of joy.

Job 8:21

Lord, I am learning that healing a broken, hurting heart is a process. As we journey from this pile of rubble in my life, give me strength to persevere. Help me not to wallow in resentment, fear, anger, or sadness. I know I need to feel my feelings, but then help me to have hope that you will give me strength to move forward. Rebuild me, Lord; realign my life with your good purposes. Help me to arise to joy and laughter again, to arise to new hope. I ask in Jesus's name. Amen.

15

When It's Hard to Wait

Prayers for Patience and Fortitude

LORD, I wait for you;
you will answer, Lord my God.

Psalm 38:15

Eleven years ago, I drove into Colorado Springs on a sunny morning in March. I was optimistic. The move from my home in the Midwest was a good thing. I was ready for a change and couldn't wait to get started on my dream of becoming a published author. I unpacked my boxes, started a new job, and began writing in my spare time. What I didn't know was that it was "seed time" in my life, not "harvest." I thought my dream would come true right away, but it didn't. I had a lot to learn about waiting and waiting well.

Over the ensuing years, I planted seeds of faith, trusting God would grow my dreams. I attended writers' conferences, joined a critique group, and read books on getting published. I prayed often, asking God to bless the work of my hands to bring hope and encouragement to others. I prayed and waited. I waited and prayed. I also obeyed, believing God as I sent letters to publishers and took steps to make contacts.

Six years later, I received a phone call from a publisher, and I was on my way to writing my first book. The seeds were beginning to sprout.

What are you waiting for—a new baby to arrive, a better job opportunity to surface, or an injury to heal? When we're young, we can't wait to grow up, and when we're grown, we're constantly looking ahead to the next chapter in life. When will I finish school? Get married? Have children? Find a better job? We always seem to be waiting for something to happen—or not happen.

Indeed, we are a society that abhors a vacuum. We want to fill life up and get what we want instantly. Perhaps it's the constant swarm of advertising that puts ideas in our heads, creating desires we never had before to want more, better, and faster. Maybe we see others who have what we want and wonder when it will be our turn. Either way, the word *wait* has gotten a bad image. Sure, it's hard to wait. And yes, it would be great if things happened according to our agenda. But there are larger forces at play.

What does God have to say about waiting—and how can we learn to do so with a joyful heart and a good attitude?

Waiting can be a time of preparation. God is getting things ready and getting us ready for his blessings. Waiting refines us; it builds character and exercises our trust muscles so they get strong and firm. God prepares, and he also finishes what he starts. So just because there is a delay does not mean the road is closed forever. As you wait, have joy, patience, and faith. "Be joyful in hope, patient in affliction, faithful in prayer" (Rom. 12:12).

Oh, if only it were that easy. When things are taking entirely too long (in *our* estimation), we may begin to take matters into our own hands and take control. But when we do, there are consequences. For example, if you put a cake in the oven and remove it before the right time, you get a hot, gooey mess. If you'd have waited, you'd have a succulent, freshly baked cake. Waiting makes a world of difference.

When things seem to be taking entirely too long, the temptation to control can be strong. But we have a choice—control or surrender. We can choose to take our hands off and allow God to work on our behalf, trusting he will come through. That takes courage; it takes faith. Thankfully, God is faithful. When we ask, he will give us the strength to do the hard things. His best is worth waiting for.

When God Delays

Because God is God and we are not, it's often hard to understand his timing or his ways. But he has reasons for delays, reasons we know not of. In John 11, we read of a time when Jesus delayed, and the results proved bigger than anyone could have anticipated.

When Jesus learned that the brother of his two friends Mary and Martha was sick, he stayed in the town where he was two days longer. The disciples who were with him probably thought it odd because they knew Jesus loved his friends—and had the power to heal. Why didn't he go to them? His followers could not have imagined how God would use this holy delay to show his glory in a most amazing way.

Finally, Jesus and his disciples went to Bethany. By the time they arrived, Lazarus was already dead. Jesus talked to the sisters and asked them where Lazarus had been laid. They showed him the place—a cave with a stone across the entrance. Jesus asked that the stone be removed. Martha protested at first because the body had been in there for four days, and there would be a stench. Undeterred, Jesus replied, "Did I not tell you that if you believe, you will see the glory of God?" (John 11:40). What happened next rocked the neighborhood, so much so that we're still talking about the event today:

So they took away the stone. Then Jesus looked up and said, "Father, I thank you that you have heard me. I knew that you always hear me, but I said this for the benefit of the people standing here, that they may believe that you sent me."

When he had said this, Jesus called in a loud voice, "Lazarus, come out!" The dead man came out, his hands and feet wrapped with strips of linen, and a cloth around his face. Jesus said to them, "Take off the grave clothes and let him go." (John 11:41–44)

No longer dead, their brother was now fully alive! Jesus could have healed the man, but the delay gave greater glory to God as Lazarus was brought back to life.

Waiting Well

Whether you're waiting for a check in the mail or an answer from your doctor's office, waiting is a part of life. How can you learn to wait well?

Know on whom you wait. The active part of waiting is learning to trust God, to rely totally on the fact that he will come through for you. It's not the answer, the thing, or the person on whom you wait; it's the Lord you wait on to deliver you. Any other way and you will be disappointed.

Wait with hope. You can choose your attitude: to fret or to have faith and wait with confident expectation. Ask God to help you with your outlook; ask him for patience and peace. As you wait, God is building in you strength, courage, fortitude, and stamina. "I wait for the LORD, my whole being waits, and in his word I put my hope" (Ps. 130:5).

Pray and obey. Waiting is not a time to do nothing. It's a time to pray and to act—to be about the Father's business. You don't have to hold all of your emotions inside; share your disappointment and frustrations with the Lord as you pray. Talk openly and honestly. And follow his lead. We wait in hope, believing even when we cannot see.

Surrender and hold on. Appreciate where you are in the process. Small beginnings can yield large results when you surrender your will—and your hopes and dreams—to God's will. Release your fears and your need to control the outcome. When you *release* what you're holding on to so tightly, *hold on* to the hope of Christ—the one who will never let you go.

Remember what God has done in the past. Peace comes and fear subsides as you look back on what God has done in the past—for those in the Bible, for others, and for you. Remind yourself that God *has* worked, *is* working, and *will* continue to work. Psalm 68:28 says, "Summon your power, God; show us your strength, our God, as you have done before."

Live in the now. Where is your focus? Are you looking so far into the future that you're dropping the ball on what's happening today? Have hope for the future, but keep your eyes on what you are doing and who you are becoming in the present.

When the Time Had Fully Come

Rachel is a single mom with toddler twins. She is also a recovered drug addict. For years she had wanted to own her own home and provide a stable life for her children. But the dream seemed entirely out of reach.

She had been watching a TV program for several months that provided an opportunity for people who had never owned a home to have their own property. So Rachel submitted an online essay to the TV show, sharing her recovery story and her longing to provide a better life for her kids. When she hit "enter" on the computer keyboard, she prayed and told God that she would trust him no matter what the response. She also prayed that God would provide for her family.

Soon Rachel learned the good news. They'd won the house! It was fully furnished, with the down payment and the first year's mortgage paid in full. Rachel said it has changed her family's life in many positive ways. To her surprise, the grateful young mom also won a new car the following year. Rachel was overwhelmed by and thankful for God's amazing provision in her life.

Ecclesiastes 3:11 says, "He has made everything beautiful in its time." In God's timing, things happen. Winter's snowy blasts turn to fragrant spring blossoms. The baby is delivered. He finally proposes. Your husband returns from military deployment. You get the job. Someday arrives.

As you wait, remember that this season will not last forever. One day things will get better—whether in this life or the next. In the meantime, have courage. Have faith. God is in control, and his timing is perfect. We may not always know the reasons for delay, or like them, but we can trust that God is working all things together for good—and for his glory.

Take your hands off, release control, and trust God. "The one who calls you is faithful, and he will do it" (1 Thess. 5:24).

A Lesson from a Bamboo Plant

Bamboo plants grow tall, but first they grow deep. When you plant a bamboo seed, it seems as if nothing is happening, nothing at all—for four years. Finally, in the fifth year, the bamboo plant shoots up a whopping eighty feet! Such incredible growth could not have been possible without the extensive root system created during those first formative years—a strong support to hold the growth that was coming. Don't give up just because you don't see any movement in your life. Know that God is at work, always at work, behind the scenes. Have faith. God's timing is perfect—in his creation and in your life.

WAITING WITH EXPECTANT HOPE

And so after waiting patiently, Abraham received what was promised.

Hebrews 6:15

Lord, I have been waiting a long time. I get tired and wonder when things will ever change. Abraham was a man who waited decades to receive what was promised to him. You told him his wife would bear him a son, even in her sunset years. And the promise was fulfilled. Help me to have faith that you will take care of my needs as you did for the fathers of our faith. I put my hope in you, loving Lord. In Jesus's name. Amen.

WAITING ON GOD, NOT PEOPLE OR THINGS

I wait for the LORD, my whole being waits,
   and in his word I put my hope.

Psalm 130:5

Lord, sometimes I lose focus and put my hope in the thing I want—a relationship, a house, a job, or something else. If only I had that, I would be happy. But I need to learn to wait on you, not the thing I long for or the person I desire. Teach me to wait on you, to look to you—firm and focused. You promise to take care of me, and I will trust that you will. I ask for your very best in this situation. Help me to wait well. In Jesus's name. Amen.

TRUSTING WHEN I DO NOT UNDERSTAND

"For my thoughts are not your thoughts,
   neither are your ways my ways," declares the LORD.

Isaiah 55:8

Lord, you amaze me. So many times I think I know what I want or need, but you know better. Your thoughts are not like mine—and that's a good thing. You know best. And I need to trust you even when I want to have things my way. I am thankful that you see the

149

bigger picture; with your bird's-eye view you protect me from things I don't even know are coming. You guide and direct and keep me on the good path. Thank you! Help me to trust your ways even when I do not understand them. I ask in Jesus's name. Amen.

GOD'S PERFECT TIMING

He has made everything beautiful in its time.

Ecclesiastes 3:11

Lord, I need patience to trust in your perfect timing. Please give me peace and endurance as I wait on your best for me in this situation. I need to remember that in your timing things ripen and ready. I don't want to grab ahold of this dream too soon and ruin it, like eating a green banana and getting a stomachache. No, I need the courage to wait. I surrender to your timing, knowing that at the right time—at your appointed time—things will be beautiful, good, and right. Help me to trust that. In Jesus's mighty name. Amen.

DON'T LOSE HEART

Therefore we do not lose heart. Though outwardly we are wasting away, yet inwardly we are being renewed day by day. For our light and momentary troubles are achieving for us an eternal glory that far outweighs them all. So we fix our eyes not on what is seen, but on what is unseen, since what is seen is temporary, but what is unseen is eternal.

2 Corinthians 4:16–18

Lord, I don't know if I can do this anymore. I feel like I have been waiting forever. I've misplaced my confidence, and I need to find hope again. Will you help me? I have been looking all around— at people, things, and circumstances—instead of straight ahead at you. Help me to see with new eyes and believe that you have more—infinitely more—for me. Renew me, Lord. I ask in Jesus's name. Amen.

TRUST IN GOD'S FAITHFUL HEART

The one who calls you is faithful, and he will do it.

1 Thessalonians 5:24

Lord, I want to believe your words are true, not just for other people but for me. I have tried and failed to make things happen on my own. I have forged ahead and taken matters into my own hands when you've said, "Wait." I am sorry. I will pray and trust that you will come through because you are the faithful God. You make promises and keep them. You said you will do it, and I am trusting that you will. Give me courage to wait for your will in your way and timing. I ask in Jesus's name. Amen.

THE LORD IS MY STRENGTH

The LORD is my strength and my shield;
    my heart trusts in him, and he helps me.
My heart leaps for joy,
    and with my song I praise him.

Psalm 28:7

Lord, in this time of waiting, I am so glad to know that you are my strength. You are my protection, and you are the one I can trust in and rely on completely. Thank you! Teach me to wait with joy and hope. Give me peace as I trust in your perfect timing. Help me to spend more time praising you than complaining. You are my source of joy. And I choose to praise you. Be my strength. In Jesus's mighty and powerful name. Amen.

GOD WILL MAKE A WAY

See, I am doing a new thing!
    Now it springs up; do you not perceive it?
I am making a way in the wilderness
    and streams in the wasteland.

Isaiah 43:19

Lord, it's been a long time, and I am still waiting for things to change in my situation. I feel like my answer has been blocked. Please remove the obstacles that are keeping me from realizing this dream. Help me to move forward whether this ever happens or not. I take comfort in the fact that you can do anything. You are God—powerful and holy, majestic and mighty, yet also loving and compassionate to your children. Today, I need a miracle. Please make a way when there seems to be no way things will change. I put my trust in you. I ask, believing in Jesus's name. Amen.

16

When You Feel Distant from God

Prayers to Come Closer

I pray that the eyes of your heart may be enlightened
in order that you may know the hope to which he has
called you.

Ephesians 1:18

Jim was brought up in a Christian home by parents who loved God and took him and his siblings to church every Sunday. He even went to hear Billy Graham speak when the popular evangelist came to his hometown. But the seed of God's words never formed deep, solid roots, and today Jim is a man who is far from God. He still circles around Christianity, but his form of religion is more like a visit to a cafeteria. He picks and chooses beliefs like some people select cake or pie.

He is what some call a *prodigal*, a person who is reckless in a very extravagant way. You may have heard about another prodigal son, in the Bible story in Luke 15. A man had two sons. The younger son asked his father for his share of the estate (which is like asking your parents for your inheritance before they've passed away—not a nice thing to do). He left home, went to a far-off country, and squandered all of his money in wild living. When his resources had run dry, there was a famine. Because he was hungry, he got a job feeding pigs. But even then no one fed him.

One day he had an idea. He'd go back home, and, though he had hurt and wronged his father, he'd ask to be one of the hired hands. At least that way he would get meals every day. He'd confess all he had done wrong and would live out his days as a servant. So he got up and started back for his hometown.

And wouldn't you know. As the son was walking down the road—still a long way off—his father ran to him, enfolded him in a hug, and kissed him. Dad must have been watching for his boy.

The amazing part is how the father greeted his son when they met on the road. The young man must have been surprised when his dad treated him with kindness instead of contempt. The father said, "Quick! Bring the best robe and put it on him. Put a ring on his finger and sandals on his feet. Bring the fattened calf and kill it. Let's have a feast and celebrate. For this son of mine was dead and is alive again; he was lost and is found" (Luke 15:22–24).

What a reaction! Startling kindness. Generous mercy. A forgiving heart. Did you know that God the Father is like that? He is not condemning. He doesn't yell at you and remind you of all you've done wrong. True, he is a God of justice—his heart breaks when we do wrong—but he is also a God of deep mercy, welcoming home his wayward sons and daughters.

Do you know someone who has strayed from the faith? Are you—or someone you care about—a prodigal child? Or maybe you've never met God the Father in the first place. Either way, you can come home. The God of grace is waiting for you.

Maybe you don't feel like you're a prodigal as such. You never ran away or lived wildly. But you don't feel as close to God as you'd like. Life just got busy. Or for some unknown reason, the most important relationship in your life slipped away. Grace and a more connected relationship with God are waiting for you as well.

A Lesson from a Waterfall

Waterfalls are beautiful. The tallest in the world, Angel Falls in Venezuela, stands at a majestic 3,212 feet. Some waterfalls cascade over naturally tiered and jagged rock formations, creating fascinating and beautiful patterns as the water falls to earth. Others fall in one long, continuous stream. They can be a relaxing and tranquil sight or, like Niagara Falls, a source of energy. No matter what their surroundings or location, most waterfalls have a continual flow and a source, the headwaters. When we are feeling lost or far from God, we can go back to the Source, the starting place—God Almighty—from whom all else flows. He is the headwaters in our lives, the origin of natural and spiritual life. When we get in the flow, he supplies the power we need to live. From the Source we receive a continual flow of love, grace, and mercy that never stops. God's living water refreshes us, and with that refreshment, we can nourish those around us, bringing hope and beauty to a thirsty world.

PRAYER FOR SALVATION

If you declare with your mouth, "Jesus is Lord," and believe in your heart that God raised him from the dead, you will be saved.

Romans 10:9

Lord, I need you. I ask for forgiveness of sinful and selfish ways. I have been wrong, and I am sorry. I believe that Jesus Christ is the Son of God and that you raised him from the dead so I could live. He was

*broken so I could be made whole. Thank you for that amazing gift!
Thank you for your love for me. I ask you to come into my heart so I
can be saved and live forever—forgiven and free. I love you; I choose
you. In Jesus's name. Amen.*

I CELEBRATE MY SALVATION

Therefore, if anyone is in Christ, the new creation has come:
The old has gone, the new is here!

2 Corinthians 5:17

*Lord, thank you for the gift of my salvation. I want to celebrate all you
have done to bring me from darkness to light. I am saved by grace—by
your mercy—not by any works of my own hands. Thank you! Now
all the angels in heaven are rejoicing because I have chosen you. I
am grateful that the old has gone and the new has come. Empower
and encourage me in this new life, the best life, as I seek to know you
more and serve you with joy. In Jesus's name. Amen.*

PRAYER FOR A PRODIGAL

Those who know your name trust in you,
    for you, O LORD, do not abandon those who search for
        you.

Psalm 9:10 NLT

*Lord, you know my heart. You see the pain I have because this person
I care about doesn't know you or isn't close to you any longer. But
you never give up hope; you never abandon anyone. Like a good
shepherd, you go to the lost sheep and bring back the one who has
strayed. Bring back my lost loved one. I ask in the mighty name and
power of Jesus. Amen.*

I WANT TO COME CLOSER

Come near to God and he will come near to you.

James 4:8

Lord, sometimes I feel so far away from you. I know I don't need to live by my feelings; the truth is you are always here. Your presence is with me. Yet I long for more closeness. I choose to come near; I choose to put you first and seek you. And your Word says that when I seek you I will find you when I search for you with all my heart. So here I am, coming, believing—despite my fears, doubts, and failures. In Jesus's name. Amen.

POWER TO CHANGE

Yours, LORD, is the greatness and the power
    and the glory and the majesty and the splendor,
      for everything in heaven and earth is yours.
Yours, LORD, is the kingdom;
    you are exalted as head over all.

1 Chronicles 29:11

Lord, I need help. I want to change, but it's not easy. So I come before you asking and praising you. You are the great and mighty God. You work miracles. You can do anything. And everything belongs to you. I praise you not just to get something from you but because you are worthy! I surrender my needs to your hands. And I praise you no matter the outcome. In Jesus's name. Amen.

FIND ME, LORD

"You will seek me and find me when you seek me with all your heart. I will be found by you," declares the LORD.

Jeremiah 29:13–14

Lord, I have been distant from you, and I am sorry. I don't know how this happened. But something inside me has been changing lately. I miss you, like a friend who has been away for a long time. You say that if I seek you I will find you. So here I am, looking, seeking, and walking your way. Let me feel peace in the comfort of your presence again. I ask in Jesus's name. Amen.

WHERE PEACE IS FOUND

Let the peace of Christ rule in your hearts. . . . And be thankful.

Colossians 3:15

Lord, everyone is looking for peace. We have restless hearts and often look in the wrong places for what only you can give—peace that is real and lasting. May the peace of God rest in me, serene and calm. And Lord, on days when my household is anything but tranquil, may I retain peace inside as I go about my day. I am so grateful for this gift of settled joy. Thank you. In Jesus's name. Amen.

RENEW MY MIND

Do not conform to the pattern of this world, but be transformed by the renewing of your mind. Then you will be able to test and approve what God's will is—his good, pleasing and perfect will.

Romans 12:2

Lord, I have not been in a good place lately. I need to know you more. I want to know you for who you really are, not who I've thought you were. The world tries to mislead me with lies that this or that will make me happy, but it never lasts. I want true peace, real joy, and total forgiveness. Renew my mind; change me, Lord. I ask in Jesus's name. Amen.

17

When You Have Health Concerns

Prayers for Healing

Give me relief from my distress;
have mercy on me and hear my prayer.

Psalm 4:1

We all know someone who needs healing from an illness, injury, or other type of health concern. We may need it for ourselves. How can we pray more effectively, even when we are in pain or suffering?

Lisa was diagnosed with rheumatoid arthritis at age twenty-four and has lived with it for more than eighteen years. It came on suddenly; within a week she went from being a perfectly healthy young woman to barely being able to open a car door or walk across a room. Her feet have broken down, her shoulders are disintegrating, and she's had four hand surgeries. Thankfully, medications have helped slow the progression of the disease, but she has never experienced remission or a day without pain in some part of her body.

Early on, Lisa felt called to reach out to those with chronic illness. She always felt that God had a plan for her pain. Today, as the founder and director of Rest Ministries (www.restministries .com), a nonprofit ministry for those with chronic illness, she is helping thousands of people who feel confused, lonely, or isolated. "I would love some pain-free days," says Lisa, "and yet every bit of pain I am in has purpose, so I can surrender my own desires back to God for my comfort." Her prayer is, "Lord, use my pain; don't let any of it go to waste!"

Her attitude amazes me as she provides hope, encouragement, and helpful resources to those in need. She encourages others rather than whining about unanswered prayers. Her mission is to share what she has learned in her suffering. She tells people that God has not forgotten them and that he offers strength in weakness. She talks about the importance of worshiping God for *who* he is, not what he can *do* for you.

It's a change in perspective when we come to realize how God works *through* our suffering, not only *after* the suffering. Lisa asks God for strength, a lessening of pain, or the ability to do something special, such as taking her son shopping for school clothes or going on a trip. She has prayed, asking God to slow the disease's progression, to help her find the right medications, to help her feel well enough to be a mom, and to enjoy life. Some days these prayers are answered; many times they are not.

Lisa shares with open honesty, "Pain can take over every thought and every emotion; it can put us into a pit of despair." But if we are willing to take the difficult step of seeking God within this pain, she continues, we can say to him, "Lord, I don't have anything left to give, but I am yours. You have me completely at your mercy." And in the midst of our situation, we can cultivate an intimacy with the Lord we never dreamed possible—a greater closeness with God because of the physical pain.

Living above Pain as You Live in It

Hezekiah was a king who lived a long time ago. As the king of Judah, he became ill and was near death. So he prayed, " 'Remember, LORD, how I have walked before you faithfully and with whole-hearted devotion and have done what is good in your eyes.' And Hezekiah wept bitterly" (Isa. 38:3).

God heard his prayers, saw his tears, and answered. The prophet Isaiah was the one to deliver the good news that God said he would add fifteen years to the king's life (Isa. 38:4–5).

In the New Testament, we read many verses about the healings and miracles Jesus performed for the sick and needy people of his day. Matthew 9:1–8 tells the story of the paralyzed man Jesus healed. He gave him not only the ability to walk again but also something he was not expecting: forgiveness.

God's power was displayed as Jesus healed blind people so they could see (see Matt. 21:14). Imagine never being able to see the beauty of God's creation or the face of a loved one. Sight restored is an amazing gift. Crowds swarmed the Son of God, and Jesus had compassion on them and healed the sick (see Matt. 14:14). Grab your Bible, look up verses about healing and restoration, and pray about your own situation.

As you pray for physical and emotional health and healing for yourself or another, here are some things to consider.

Ask for what you need. Do you need money for medical bills? Do you need strength to get out of bed each day? Ask God in prayer. Be expectant and have a positive attitude. You don't know how God will answer or when. But you can always have hope—hope in the Lord, not in your circumstances.

When we come to God in prayer, we are to ask in Jesus's name (John 14:13); lean on the Lord, not our own understanding (Prov. 3:5–6); pray for God's will to be done (Matt. 6:10); and ask according to his will (1 John 5:14).

Develop great faith. How can we strengthen our faith in God? As we saturate ourselves with the words of God—by reading the Bible, meditating on it, and hearing it over and over again—our faith gets fed. Saturate means to drench or inundate yourself with God's words. It does not mean sprinkling a few drops here and there. That would be like putting a teaspoon of gasoline in your car and wondering why it doesn't work. You need to fill up the entire tank so the car runs the way it was intended to. Pray and ask God to strengthen your faith.

Have patience. Healing may come right away, but most often it takes time. We need to remember that God's timetable is not like ours. For some, healing may not happen in this lifetime. That's where hope comes in, the hope that one day pain and suffering will end. In the meantime, ask God what he wants you to learn from this illness or injury. Seek to find purpose each day despite pain or limitations, and you will find yourself coming closer to God in unexpected and glorious ways.

Live in the mystery. What about when we pray and healing does not come? We may think, *If God is loving and he cares about me, why doesn't he take away this pain? Why doesn't he heal me?* These are valid questions, to be sure.

We live in the mystery that God is wiser than we are. He knows what he is doing, and one day—when we are with him either here on earth or in heaven—we will be forever free from all pain and suffering. Today, we don't know the answer, but we choose to keep on trusting. "Trust in the LORD with all your heart and lean not on your own understanding; in all your ways submit to him, and he will make your paths straight. Do not be wise in your own eyes; fear the LORD and shun evil. This will bring health to your body and nourishment to your bones" (Prov. 3:5–8).

We live in a broken, fallen world. We can, as my friend Judy, a hospice chaplain, says, "live *above* the suffering as we live *in* it." We live above our pain as we look first to Christ. We live above it as we find daily encouragement from the Word and daily distrac-

162

tions to keep our mind off our situation, like gazing at the beauty of God's creation—the glory of an ocean sunset, a momma deer and her little ones on the front lawn, or a gentle snowfall on tall pine trees. "We live above the pain of the moment by living in the hope that one day God will set all things right," Judy says.

Whether it's a physical or an emotional ailment, we know that, as a friend shared with me recently, "God does not cause hardship. He is with us in the hardship." Character grows in adversity, and we are being formed daily into the image of Christ. In my own life, I am grateful for all God has done and is doing regarding my health and healing. Because of past pain, I am more grateful when I have pain-free days. I don't take for granted a good night's sleep. I appreciate my health so much more.

Trust God No Matter What

After she was diagnosed with kidney failure, Ava found herself asking the question, "Can I trust and love God even in the bad times?" She had several months of dialysis, and then her father gave her life again in the form of a kidney transplant. Through that trial, Ava learned she could love and trust her heavenly Father to provide and care for her; he was faithful and gracious just as he had promised.

Fast-forward thirteen years, and Ava is sitting in the doctor's office trying to comprehend the news that she has a tumor and it has to be removed (along with a total hysterectomy). The tumor could be malignant, but the doctors aren't certain; they will know more after the surgery. Ava did not want to accept or believe that the tumor was malignant. She had many friends praying for her healing. But after the surgery, she learned that, in fact, the tumor was malignant. It was stage-four uterine cancer—a very aggressive illness requiring very aggressive treatment. Again, she found herself asking if she could trust God through another health crisis.

During the difficulties of chemotherapy and radiation, Ava listened over and over again to music with lyrics that reminded her that no matter what the outcome the Lord would be with her. At times she'd sing along at the top of her lungs; other times she'd cry so hard she couldn't utter a word.

Despite her challenging circumstances, God provided and cared for Ava through her family, friends, co-workers, and even strangers. She had too many blessings to count! Although her health issues persist, she says that she never has to ask that question again; she knows God is faithful and gracious. We can trust and love him no matter what.

In this world, we will have suffering, aches, and pains. I, for one, am going to press in and pray on. I'm going to persevere—asking, seeking, and knocking on the door of the one who loves me most. Who knows what the Lord will do? As you pray for your health concerns, *in the midst of* suffering, may you discover wild hope and never-give-up faith.

A Lesson from a Beautiful Garden

Picture this: The sky is perfectly blue, and the sun is warm on your face. The delightful fragrance of newly opened roses wafts around you as you sit amidst the vibrant colors and greenery of a beautiful garden. Research shows that "just strolling through a garden or, for that matter, seeing one out your window, can lower blood pressure, reduce stress, and ease pain."[1]

Interestingly, the article also states that "hospitals, rehabilitation centers, and nursing homes increasingly come equipped with 'healing' or 'therapeutic' gardens where patients and staff can get away from sterile, indoor surroundings. Many also offer patients a chance to get their hands dirty and their minds engaged in the nurturing work of plant care."[2]

For centuries people have found pleasure in gardening as a relaxing pastime. And for good reason. Viewing the natural beauty God created helps us to relax and replenish—and heal.

WHEN I AM IN PAIN

Have mercy on me, Lord, for I am faint;
> heal me, Lord, for my bones are in agony . . .
> for the Lord has heard my weeping.
The Lord has heard my cry for mercy;
> the Lord accepts my prayer.

Psalm 6:2, 8–9

Lord, I need you. I am in so much pain. I know that you hear my prayers and see my tears. I need your loving arms of comfort around me right now. Help me through, Lord. Please take away the pain or give me the strength to bear it. I pray that the doctors would have the wisdom to help me find relief. Help me to have faith and keep on believing in the midst of this pain. I believe you will come through for me; help me through. In Jesus's name. Amen.

JESUS HEALS THE SICK

When Jesus landed and saw a large crowd, he had compassion on them and healed their sick.

Matthew 14:14

Lord, thank you for your compassion and care for the sick. I need a healing touch on my body today. Please come to me and heal my aches and pains. Free me from my suffering. I need relief, and I need you to enter into my circumstances. I praise you. I worship you. Be with me in this hard time and give me peace. In Jesus's name. Amen.

I WANT TO BE A HEALTHIER PERSON

But for you who revere my name, the sun of righteousness
will rise with healing in its rays. And you will go out and frolic
like well-fed calves.

Malachi 4:2

Lord, I long to be a healthier person. Physically, emotionally, and spiritually, I need your healing and cleansing in my life. You are the Healer. Over and over, I read stories in your Word about how your power healed the sick, the blind, and those who could not walk. You gave them health and forgiveness of sins. I ask, believing. Will you please heal me, Lord? Help me to trust in your way, your timing, and your outcome that I may glorify you with my life. In Jesus's name. Amen.

I NEED MONEY FOR MEDICAL BILLS

And my God will meet all your needs according to the riches
of his glory in Christ Jesus.

Philippians 4:19

Lord, I come before you desperate and grateful. It's an odd combination, but I know that you are aware of my need for money to pay these mounting medical bills, and I am also thankful that you will meet the need. I don't know when or how, but in your divine providence and sovereignty, I ask that you would provide in ways I cannot even imagine. You are the Source, and I put my trust in you, Lord. I ask for provision. In Jesus's name. Amen.

SUFFERING AND FUTURE GLORY

I consider that our present sufferings are not worth
comparing with the glory that will be revealed in us.

Romans 8:18

Lord, I ask in the mighty and powerful name of Jesus that you would heal me. Take away my suffering. And in the middle of my circumstances, help me to remember that all of this pain is not for nothing because one day your glory will be revealed in me in heaven—a place of no tears and no pain, a place of extreme joy. I will see you face-to-face! Today, things are challenging; one day they will not be. Help me to hold on to hope as I put my trust in you. In Jesus's name. Amen.

LORD, RENEW MY STRENGTH

But those who hope in the LORD
    will renew their strength.
They will soar on wings like eagles;
    they will run and not grow weary,
    they will walk and not be faint.

Isaiah 40:31

Lord, when my strength is fading and my hope is running dry, please come and help me. I want to do and be so much more in this life, but my health issues tether me down when I want to soar like an eagle. My hope is in you—my Healer, my Restorer. Show me how to walk in this life, whether I find healing or not. Give me purpose and passion and the ability to live in the least amount of pain possible. In Jesus's name. Amen.

HEALTH RESTORED

LORD my God, I called to you for help,
    and you healed me.
You, LORD, brought me up from the realm of the dead;
    you spared me from going down to the pit.

Psalm 30:2–3

Lord, thank you for healing me! I am so grateful. I don't know why you chose to heal me while others still suffer—no one knows. But I do know that you are the holy God who heals. And I want to say a heartfelt thank-you. Let me live my life wisely, still trusting and depending on you. You are the one I praise. In Jesus's name. Amen.

18

When You Have Job/Career Issues

Prayers for Guidance

Whatever you do, work at it with all your heart, as
working for the Lord, not for human masters.

Colossians 3:23

The layoffs took everyone in our company by surprise.
One Friday morning last summer, my director called me
into her office. She told me that our parent company was
making nationwide layoffs, and my job was being cut. I had a few
hours to tie up loose ends and clear out my things.

Sadly, I wasn't alone. Job cuts, downsizing, layoffs, and business closings were happening all over the country. Perhaps you
can relate—or know someone who can. In the past few years, the
economy has been like a roller-coaster ride—up and down, with
unexpected twists and turns. Not only in America but across the
globe, workers in trades and careers of all kinds have known uncertainty and loss.

Maybe your tough times at work are different. There's that one person who really irks you, and you have to work closely with her. Or your boss isn't treating you well. It could be that you simply don't make enough money and don't have any prospects for another job. Or you may be starting a new job or opening a new business, and you need prayer to combat fear and find courage and success in your new opportunity.

In uncertain times, what do you do with your emotions? How do you handle the stress when there's so much to do and never enough time? If you are feeling the crushing weight of a demanding job, then pray. If you are unemployed, pray. Whatever you are facing in your job or career, talk with God about it in prayer. Hope is here—and help is just a prayer away.

Powerful Prayer

Prayer is not a magical formula to get what we want. We don't have to say things perfectly or in a certain order. Instead, God asks us to believe—to believe in him and have faith that he will come through for us. Sometimes we need to wait; other times we need to take action. In the waiting or in the activity, God's Holy Spirit gives us the power to put the Word of God into action; he enables us to have discernment, courage, and fortitude to stand strong in the midst of hard times. He increases our faith as we ask him and choose to believe.

Ask God what he has for you today. For example, if you are unemployed, try thinking of it as being "reassigned." You have a new assignment in *this* place, with *these* people, for *this* time. It could all change tomorrow, but how does God want you to best serve him today?

Tell him you want to be a man or woman of excellence in your workplace and ask him to give you insight, good ideas, and stamina to do your job both efficiently and effectively. For instance, Kelly and another clerk at her store pray weekly with the owner and ask God to bless their business with new clients—and they've shown up.

Prayer is a conversation, talking with and listening to the Lord. It doesn't have to be a *duty*; it can be a *delight* as you come to know more fully the one with whom you converse. He loves and accepts you. He listens and cares. He wants the best for you, so you can speak openly and honestly from your heart. In your prayer time, consider these things:

What do you appreciate about God? Praise him.

What are you grateful for? Thank him.

What are you sorry for? Confess to him.

What do you need? Ask him.

Powerful prayers don't necessarily have to be long and involved, but they should be heartfelt and sincere, directed to the powerful Almighty God who has the ability, resources, and desire to help you. An effective prayer can be a simple prayer. Preacher and scholar George A. Buttrick once said, "Prayer is listening as well as speaking, receiving as well as asking; and its deepest mood is friendship, held in reverence."[1]

Your own personal "happy hour," your quiet time with God, can be a holy time and a connecting time as you get to know him more. As you spend time with God, you will come to deeper depths of awe at his wonder, worship at his majesty, and acceptance of his never-ending love. Often, we want answers, but first he wants us to want him—and connect in relationship.

Life is meant to be enjoyed, not simply endured. As you pray about your work life or your ministry, remember the importance of rest and recreation too. Fun and play, adventure and exploration can reinvigorate you and, when you return, help you be more effective in your work life because you've been refreshed.

Feeling aimless? Looking for more meaning and purpose in your life calling? Talk to God and believe that he will provide for you. He

171

knows why you're here, even when you don't. He created you with a mind to think and reason, with skills and abilities, and with passions and desires. God wants you to fulfill your heart's desires and callings too. No matter what your age, it's never too late to begin anew.

Proverbs 19:21 says, "Many are the plans in a person's heart, but it is the LORD's purpose that prevails." One day, maybe soon, things will turn around. Pray on—with hope—believing God. And keep your eyes open for your answered prayer.

A Lesson from a Sparrow

You have this situation at work. It's hard. It's bugging you. And you wonder if God really cares about your work life. Perhaps you think he's too busy saving the world to be concerned about the co-worker who's driving you nuts or your heavy workload. Indeed, the one who created you cares deeply about your weekdays and your weekends. Matthew 6:26 reminds us, "Look at the birds of the air; they do not sow or reap or store away in barns, and yet your heavenly Father feeds them. Are you not much more valuable than they?" God provides for the birds of the air, even the tiniest sparrow. He will also provide, so much more so, for you.

ENTRUSTING MY WORK LIFE TO GOD

Commit to the LORD whatever you do,
and he will establish your plans.

Proverbs 16:3

Lord, thank you for my job. You are the one who opens doors and provides opportunities, and I am grateful. Refresh and revive me with your power and energy to do what I need to get done today. Give me good ideas and help me to have favor with my co-workers and our customers—those we serve every day. I commit this job to you and ask you to bless the work of my hands for your glory. In Jesus's name. Amen.

WHAT SHOULD I DO WITH MY LIFE?

The LORD God took the man and put him in the Garden of
Eden to work it and take care of it.

Genesis 2:15

*Lord, I need direction. I don't know what path to take, which job is
right for me. Long ago, you created the first man, Adam, and he was
the first gardener. He nurtured and tended the plants and flowers.
What have you equipped me to do? How can I best serve you with
my gifts and talents? Uncover the treasures you have in me and let
them bloom forth to be a blessing in my life and in the lives of those
I will serve. Thank you that you have a plan for my life. In Jesus's
name. Amen.*

BEING A LIGHT IN THE WORKPLACE

You are the light of the world. A town built on a hill cannot
be hidden. Neither do people light a lamp and put it under
a bowl. Instead they put it on its stand, and it gives light to
everyone in the house. In the same way, let your light shine
before others, that they may see your good deeds and
glorify your Father in heaven.

Matthew 5:14–16

*Lord, I want to be a bright light in my workplace. Help me to be a
person who works well and gets along with others, someone who
motivates and encourages others too. Sometimes other people try
to snuff out the light in my life with criticism, gossip, or jealousy.
May your strong and true light shine even brighter in me because
light always overcomes the darkness! Let them see Christ in me. In
Jesus's name. Amen.*

HELP FOR GETTING ALONG WITH OTHERS

God is just: He will pay back trouble to those who trouble
you.

2 Thessalonians 1:6

Lord, I need help. Sometimes I just don't understand other people. They can be so mean-spirited. They gossip and do things that really annoy me. Please help me to get along with my co-workers. Show me what I need to do differently so we can have a more peaceful place of employment. Even though we are different, help us to respect each other even when we do not agree. I ask in Jesus's name. Amen.

WHEN MY JOB IS STRESSFUL

We are hard pressed on every side, but not crushed;
perplexed, but not in despair.

2 Corinthians 4:8

Lord, I don't know if I can handle the stress of this job much longer. There is always so much to do and never enough time. Will you please help me? I don't want to live this way. But I also know that good jobs are hard to find. And yet, despite all that, I know you are bigger than my situation. You are stronger. Please show me if I should stay and help me to be energized to get my work done. Or if you have a new place for me to work—and to shine—please open doors for me. I ask, believing in Jesus's name. Amen.

WHEN I AM UNEMPLOYED

Being confident of this, that he who began a good work in you will carry it on to completion until the day of Christ Jesus.

Philippians 1:6

Lord, I need a job. I need help with finances. It's scary not knowing where the money will come from, and I fear not having enough. And yet this is not the end. You didn't bring me this far just to leave me here alone. You finish what you start—in the world and in my life. Increase my confidence and trust that you started a good work in me and will carry out your plans for my life. I am leaning on you, Jesus, clinging to you. In Jesus's name. Amen.

WORK SERVING GOD, NOT MEN

Whatever you do, work at it with all your heart, as working for the Lord, not for human masters, since you know that you will receive an inheritance from the Lord as a reward. It is the Lord Christ you are serving.

Colossians 3:23–24

Lord, help me to remember as I go about my workday that it's you I serve and not man. I will do my best by the empowerment you provide, and I will strive for excellence and give respect to my boss. But, ultimately, you are the one I am working for, the one I serve and want to please. I run this race of life, eyes on the prize, leaning on you. Help me, Lord. In Jesus's name. Amen.

19

When You Have Relationship Issues

Prayers for Wisdom

Live in harmony with one another.

Romans 12:16

Chloe and Jason had been on two adoption agency waiting lists for nearly five years (for a boy from India and a girl from China). Chloe had been looking forward to the days when she would travel with her husband to both countries to pick up their new son and daughter. She had rehearsed in her mind those two special days when she'd hold each of these precious children in her arms for the first time. She longed for them with a mother's heart and anticipated the moments.

Then, right before they were preparing to travel, Chloe realized she was pregnant. It was a blessing from God, indeed, but she was too sick to travel and disappointed that she wouldn't be able to go on either adventure.

Thankfully, her husband's family rallied behind them during this unexpected twist of events. Jason's dad went with him to China to pick up their new daughter, and his brother took off work and left his family to travel with Jason to India to get their new son. His entire extended family got excited about the two adoptions in a new way. They all wanted photos of the newly adopted kids and couldn't wait to hear the latest news about each travel adventure. A special bond developed between their Chinese daughter and her grandpa that probably wouldn't have happened if he hadn't traveled to China to pick her up with Jason. The little boy also has a special bond with his grandma because of the time spent with her upon his arrival in America.

In a strange way, Chloe is thankful she wasn't able to travel to China or India. Sometimes, she says, our unanswered prayers lead us closer to what we truly need. In the midst of a difficult time, God revealed the power of community, family, and how much we really do need one another.

Created for Relationships

We were created for relationships of all kinds—family, friends, co-workers, neighbors, and others. Every day we come into contact with people, from the pizza delivery guy to the receptionist at work. We see people at church, in social groups, or at community activities.

Sometimes the interactions are enjoyable; other times there are misunderstandings and stress. The fact is that where there are relationships, there is bound to be conflict. How do we handle tough times? How do we learn to get along, build deeper connections, get through life's challenges, and find hope? How can we cherish what we have, serve each other in love, and be thankful?

No matter what the relationship or connection—or disconnection—there is hope for healing when we come to God in prayer.

When we have a right relationship with God, our primary and most important connection, it helps improve our relationships with others. When we pray, God can empower us to speak words that are kind and to treat others with love and respect. Words are powerful; they can bless or hurt people.

Love One Another

The Bible doesn't have a "how to treat people well" section, but throughout Scripture God reveals how to act toward one another in all kinds of relationships. Ephesians 4:32 reminds us to be kind and compassionate and to forgive each other. First Peter 3:8 admonishes us to be sympathetic and humble. Here are a few other passages from the Bible that tell us how to live wisely and well in the context of relationships:

> "Live in harmony with one another" (Rom. 12:16).
> "Therefore let us stop passing judgment on one another" (Rom. 14:13).
> "Love one another deeply, from the heart" (1 Pet. 1:22).
> "Accept one another, then, just as Christ accepted you" (Rom. 15:7).
> "Therefore encourage one another and build each other up" (1 Thess. 5:11).

Sound like a tall order? In our own strength, yes. But as we pray, God can enable us to do what we cannot do on our own.

Of all the relationships we have in life, our most important relationship is with God. And the way we connect with him is through prayer, praise, and worship. It's a relationship we maintain for the rest of our lives—and beyond. Prayer is a partnership; we are the hands and feet to accomplish God's purposes.

A strong spiritual foundation is formed through consistent prayer and, especially in difficult times, helps us stand strong. The prayer-filled life is a powerful life; it is a surrendered life (a continual dying to self and arising to follow God's ways); and it is a joy-filled life.

No matter what your relationship struggles, God will help you through when you put your hope in him.

A Lesson from the Ocean Waves

Walking along a sandy beach is a favorite pastime for many people. They love to walk barefoot and feel the water wash across their feet as the ocean waves roll in and out. It's interesting how the ocean waves know when to stop. They reach the beach and retreat. In fact, God designed it that way. "This far you may come and no farther; here is where your proud waves halt" (Job 38:11).

But watch out for wind gusts, because this place of beauty can soon become a place of destruction. With a few gale-force winds, gigantic waves form with tremendous power and force. Instead of gently lapping along the coastline, these larger, crashing waves can cause damage to the ecosystems and communities along the coast. In nature and in relationships, we need boundaries. Otherwise, damage can occur.

Some people are like large waves; they crash (or attempt to crash) the landscape of your heart with harmful words or actions. Like a destructive tidal wave, they wreak havoc in the lives of everyone in their path. But love needs limits; that's true freedom. Do you know your limits—the emotional and physical boundaries of what you will and will not accept from others? Do they?

WHEN I HAVE OFFENDED OTHERS

Search me, God, and know my heart;
    test me and know my anxious thoughts.

See if there is any offensive way in me,
and lead me in the way everlasting.

Psalm 139:23–24

Lord, I come before you. I'm having a hard time in a certain relationship. Yet before I ask you to change him or her, I need to check my own heart first. Is there anything I am doing wrong? Is there something I've done that is offensive and hurting the situation? Bring to mind how I can change and be different. Lord, forgive me. Help me to be right with you and with this other person. I ask for healing in our relationship. I value the relationship and need your help. In Jesus's name. Amen.

ACCEPT ONE ANOTHER

Accept one another, then, just as Christ accepted you, in order to bring praise to God.

Romans 15:7

Lord, people are so different from each other. Some people have lifestyles or make choices that conflict with my own. And yet you call me to accept others just as they are. I don't always have to agree with or like their choices, but I pray for a heart of understanding—even when I do not understand. You have accepted me; help me to be accepting of others to bring glory to your name. In Jesus's name. Amen.

LOVE IN ACTION

Dear children, let us not love with words or speech but with actions and in truth.

1 John 3:18

Lord, teach me about love so I can be a more loving person. You tell me that love is not only about the words I say but also about what I do; my actions matter. Help me to speak words that are kind and encouraging. Help my actions to reflect love. I want to live a life of love, to model it for others and to receive it in return. I ask in Jesus's name. Amen.

HONORING MY PARENTS

"Honor your father and mother"—which is the first commandment with a promise—"so that it may go well with you and that you may enjoy long life on the earth."

Ephesians 6:2–3

Lord, thank you for my parents. Whether we get along or not, help me to honor my mother and my father with my words and actions. You promised that when we respect and honor the ones who raised us, it will go well in our own lives. Show me how best to honor my parents with kindness and truth—even if it's with a phone call, a short note, or a visit. I choose to obey you. Teach us how to love each other in ways we can each receive and be blessed. In Jesus's name. Amen.

PRAYER FOR SINGLES

Trust in the LORD with all your heart
　　and lean not on your own understanding;
in all your ways submit to him,
　　and he will make your paths straight.

Proverbs 3:5–6

Lord, I ask for a good attitude and discernment in this stage of my life and always. I ask for contentment as I pursue the path you have for me today. If you have someone for me to marry, please show me your will clearly—and reveal it to the other person. Give me peace as I wait on your timing for connecting our lives as husband and wife. I surrender my desires. Protect me from unhealthy relationships and save me for your very best. Keep my future spouse in your care. Whether I marry one day or stay single, give me courage to trust you with all my heart. Help me not to miss all that you have for me in this life. In Jesus's name. Amen.

PRAYER FOR MARRIAGE

Follow God's example, therefore, as dearly loved children
and walk in the way of love, just as Christ loved us and gave
himself up for us as a fragrant offering and sacrifice to God.

Ephesians 5:1–2

*Lord, I ask that you would bless our marriage in the name and power
of Jesus. Help us to walk in the way of love. May we have mutual af-
fection and respect for each other, giving of our time and attention
in ways the other person can receive. Teach us how to communicate
well. Help us to balance work and family responsibilities. Keep strong
our passion and care for each other. Give us patience to respect our
differences, and when conflict or hard times come, help us to stay
connected and forgive readily. Centered on you, Lord, may we both
keep choosing you every day and choosing each other. Bless our love,
Lord. In Jesus's name. Amen.*

PRAYER FOR FAMILY

Therefore, as God's chosen people, holy and dearly loved,
clothe yourselves with compassion, kindness, humility,
gentleness and patience. Bear with each other and forgive
one another if any of you has a grievance against someone.
Forgive as the Lord forgave you. And over all these virtues
put on love, which binds them all together in perfect unity.

Colossians 3:12–14

*Lord, I ask that you would bless each person in our household and our
extended family. May our home be a place where love lives. Despite
our differences, help us to respect one another and not demand our
own way, forgive one another and not hold grudges. Show us how
to live in peace and harmony, serving one another with love. Bless
our family, Lord. Give us wisdom in teaching wisdom to our children,
with love and discipline. Help our family to be connected and enjoy
one another. No matter what the circumstances, let this be a place
of life, love, and laughter—as we lean on you. In Jesus's name. Amen.*

PRAYER FOR A WIDOW OR WIDOWER

The widow who is really in need and left all alone puts her hope in God and continues night and day to pray and to ask God for help.

1 Timothy 5:5

Lord, thank you for the gift of my spouse and the years together with which you have blessed us. I am truly grateful. Life is different for me now, and it's taking time to adjust to being alone. Yet with you, Lord, I am never alone. My hope is in you. Help me to get my needs met, both in things around the house and in companionship. Give me grace to live in this new season of my life, knowing you are with me in every season. In Jesus's name. Amen.

PRAYER FOR THE DIVORCED OR SEPARATED

I lift up my eyes to the mountains—
    where does my help come from?
My help comes from the LORD,
    the Maker of heaven and earth.

Psalm 121:1–2

Lord, I ask for healing of my heart. You are my Helper and my Healer. I look to you in my time of need. It's hard getting through this time of separation and divorce; ending a marriage is painful for everyone. I am grateful that you are always here. You care about every aspect of my life, and I ask for help in this difficult time of complex emotions and myriad details. Help me through, Lord. In Jesus's name. Amen.

PRAYER FOR A SINGLE PARENT

As for me, I will always have hope;
    I will praise you more and more.

Psalm 71:14

Lord, I never planned on being in this situation, but here I am single again with children. You have been with me every step of this journey;

I know you will not fail me now. No matter what my marital status, I will cling to you, my Wild Hope. And I will praise you. Even when I do not understand, I will trust you. Give me the fortitude and the faith to raise my kids, to do well at my job, and to cling to you for hope and strength. Thank you for all you have done for me. In Jesus's name. Amen.

STRENGTHEN MY FRIENDSHIPS

A friend loves at all times.

Proverbs 17:17

Lord, thank you for my friends. What a blessing it is to have people who know me well and care about my life. Please strengthen my friendships and make them solid and lasting. Show me how I can best care for those I care about. And Lord, at times in my life when I need more friends—or closer ones—will you please meet the need? Teach me how to be a good friend to others and to find fulfillment in the relationships I am developing. In Jesus's name. Amen.

PRAYING FOR OTHERS I MEET

Live in harmony with one another. Do not be proud, but be willing to associate with people of low position. Do not be conceited.

Romans 12:16

Lord, I run into many people in the course of my life, people who need an encouraging word or a smile, like those with whom I interact at the dry cleaners, the hardware store, or my daughter's ballet class. You love all people, and I am called to be like you. Help me to be a person who is kind to others, no matter who they are. Help me to live in harmony and be a peacemaker so your name will be glorified. In Jesus's name. Amen.

20

When You Have Money Issues

Prayers for Financial Help

And my God will meet all your needs according to the
riches of his glory in Christ Jesus.

Philippians 4:19

Kim and Gary had moved their family half a world away,
from their native Nebraska to Sydney, Australia, in order
for Gary to pursue a degree in worship and creative arts.
They had carefully saved and budgeted prior to leaving the States
so they would have enough money to take them through the two-
year course.

Shortly after they arrived in Australia, the exchange rate took
a downturn, and their money didn't stretch as far as they'd anticipated. The couple learned that the government wouldn't allow
them to work more than twenty hours per week, and the cost of
living was more than they had anticipated. Within eight months,
their savings had dried up.

It was terribly frightening to be thousands of miles away from home with no way to leave and no way to stay. Gary and Kim began to pray.

Three weeks after they hit bottom, Kim was trying to figure out what to feed her two growing boys that would fill them up—without exhausting their extremely limited funds. A sense of desperation began to settle over her; she felt utterly hopeless. Kim cried out to God, relying totally on him to take care of her and her family.

Shortly after that, a friend came to the door. Mark had recently bought a new car, and he and his daughter wanted to show it to Kim's family. Needless to say, she wasn't very enthusiastic about seeing their beautiful red sports car sitting in her driveway when she could barely feed her children.

Kim tried to listen patiently as Mark described all of its features. She oohed and ahhed at the interior's new smell, but inside she wanted to scream. As Mark stood next to the car, he said, "You simply have to see the trunk. It's mammoth!" She smiled weakly as he popped open the "boot." Suddenly, Kim realized why he had wanted her to see his car. The trunk was filled with groceries and household goods for her family—enough to last several weeks! Kim began to cry tears of joy as Mark and his daughter carried the first of many loads into her home.

Even her children were deeply affected by Mark's generous gift, as Kim explained to them how God had answered their prayers. Kim and Gary learned unforgettable lessons in faith and provision as God showed up in amazing and unexpected ways.

Today, many families and individuals are struggling. They may be unemployed or underemployed—out of work or not making enough to make ends meet. Debt is at an all-time high, and many people—probably even some you know—are going through the heartbreak of bankruptcy or home foreclosure. Often, a lack of funds can cause untold tension and arguments between spouses.

Financial Deserts

You may feel like you are in a financial desert—it's dry and barren, with more lack than abundance. Living in a financial desert isn't only hard; it can also be embarrassing. Fear of not having enough or what other people will think can keep you up at night. Unless you have a firm grasp about what the Bible has to say about money and begin to believe it's true, your peace will be lacking and your joy will fade.

Perhaps you've heard of another desert experience, the one recorded in the Bible when Moses led the people of Israel out of slavery in Egypt and through a desert wilderness, where they wandered for forty years. You can read about it in the book of Exodus. God provided for their need for food with manna, which showed up on the ground every morning; for water, when Moses struck a rock with a rod; and for footwear, as their shoes never wore out—not for decades! During that dry time, God showed his power in great and mighty ways.

If you are in a financial desert right now, will you trust God? Will you believe like never before that he will provide for you?

Promised Land Living

Maybe you're not living in desert-dry financial times. You're in the "Promised Land" in the sense that you have enough—or more than enough—to meet your expenses. How are you balancing your spending, saving, and giving? Are you a generous giver? Are you tithing?

Sometimes the words *tithing* and *giving* can be confusing. Your tithe is the 10 percent you give to the church. Gifts are over and above your tithe, given to the church or to missions, ministries, or other organizations, like the food bank in your town.

God asks us to give our first and best, the firstfruits of our income. However, our pastor recently said that only 30 percent of people who attend church give anything at all; 70 percent give nothing. Perhaps it's because they are not aware of the concept of tithing. Or people may mistakenly think that if they can't give the full 10 percent of their income, as the Bible states, then they'll give nothing. Ten percent can seem like a lot of money when you're barely scraping by.

Giving to the church doesn't have to be an all-or-nothing proposition. Instead, give *something*, even if it's a small amount, because you are giving from your heart. Then as your income increases, you can "tithe up," as my friend Anne says, and give more. Ask God for favor and abundance so you will have more to give to others because, once you start, you will discover the joy of generosity. Giving feels good! And it helps others in need.

Faith and Finances

Years ago, I worked for a ministry that provides financial services to Christian organizations. There I learned that God owns everything (Ps. 24:1), including what we feel is "our" money. He gave us the job we have and the ability to earn an income; God gives us the ability to produce wealth (Deut. 8:18). Yet even though God owns everything, he calls us to be wise stewards or managers of our finances.

It's been said that money is one of the top three things couples argue about (the other two being sex and kids). Money can be an emotionally charged subject. Married or unmarried, we all need wisdom on how to save, spend, and give wisely. That's why powerful prayer is essential. Praying about how to handle finances is important no matter what your financial status.

When you pray, something incredible happens. You are able to release your tight grasp on money. You can be free from your heart-struggles with money. We cannot worship or serve both God and money, as we learn in Luke 16:13.

In prayer, we come to learn that money comes from God—he provides our income, and we manage the saving, spending, and giving. From our hands, it goes back to God (in tithing and giving) and meets the needs of others. There is a flow of receiving and giving. Our hearts need to be right with God so the process doesn't get clogged up, like when we try to keep all that God has given us to ourselves. When that happens, we can ask God for a right heart and a new perspective.

Whether we have plenty or lack, we can be wealthy in other ways. Your savings may be depleted, but you can be rich in love, friendship, and hope. You can be prosperous in your deep, abiding relationship with God and blessed with an abundance of close family members and friends.

If you are feeling defeated in your finances, turn to God. Ask him to help you. Confess your misconceptions about money and ask him to release anything that is holding you back or gripping your heart in this area. Have hope that one day there will be *more than enough*—beyond what you can ask or imagine.

God loves to surprise and delight his children. When I was in the desert of financial hard times a few years ago, I was amazed at how God provided. I didn't expect it or ask for it. Friends provided generously, whether it was a check, groceries, a TV, a microwave—even kind words of encouragement. And God? He gave me everything. He prompted the hearts of my friends to help their hurting friend in her time of desperate need.

Have courage. Have faith. When all seems hopeless, Jesus Christ is your Wild Hope—and mine.

A Lesson from an Acorn

You may have heard the familiar expression "Big oaks from little acorns grow." It always amazes me when I look at an acorn how a tall tree can come from such a small seed. But nothing will happen unless it is first surrendered to the soil. Release precedes growth. Likewise, when we surrender our hearts and our attitude toward money to God, growth happens. In the black soil of faith, God grows our character and integrity tall and strong. When we ask, he can give us wisdom on how to save, spend, and give from all that he has provided and given to us. Ask God for "acorn faith" to plant seeds of hope for what he will do in your finances. Ask him for wise management of your money so it will bear fruit—in your own life and in the lives of those in need.

MONEY VERSUS THE LOVE OF MONEY

Keep your lives free from the love of money and be
content with what you have, because God has said,
"Never will I leave you; never will I forsake you."

Hebrews 13:5

Lord, help me to have a clear view on money. I need it to pay my bills, get what I need, and help others. But I don't want to be in bondage to the love of money or be greedy. I want to trust you to provide for all I need and find freedom in that. Instead of striving continually for more stuff, let me be satisfied with what I have. Help me to be wise in my attitude toward money and how I manage my finances. You are first. Always first. In Jesus's name. Amen.

LORD, I'M BROKE

Hear me, Lord, and answer me,
for I am poor and needy.

Psalm 86:1

Lord, I need help. I never seem to have enough money. I feel like I am always just barely scraping by, and I am tired. I am ashamed and embarrassed. I need hope. Please meet my needs with your amazing resources. I come to you believing by faith that you will come through for me. I don't know how or when, but I know you will. And I am grateful that you hear me and will answer me. I ask in Jesus's name. Amen.

HELP IN TIMES OF TROUBLE

Then call on me when you are in trouble,
and I will rescue you,
and you will give me glory.

Psalm 50:15 NLT

Lord, my finances are a mess. You know the situation; you know how hard it has been for me. So here I am trusting you to make a way where there seems to be no way out. I surrender my agenda, my budget, and how I think things should happen. I let go and give you my financial burden. I ask for favor not just to get by but to find victory in my finances—to have more than enough and to get ahead! In hard times or good times, I will trust you. In Jesus's name. Amen.

GIVING FROM THE HEART

Each of you should give what you have decided in your heart to give, not reluctantly or under compulsion, for God loves a cheerful giver.

2 Corinthians 9:7

Lord, thank you for your provision and for all that you've given me. I am truly blessed. I ask for wisdom to know how much I should give and to which ministries or individuals. You know my heart, and I pray that I will be a cheerful giver, openhanded and joyful about all you have done for me. I ask that you would continue to supply my needs so I can keep helping others. In Jesus's name. Amen.

GOD WILL PROVIDE FOR ME

Every good and perfect gift is from above, coming down from the Father of the heavenly lights, who does not change like shifting shadows.

James 1:17

Lord, what a blessing it is to know that you provide for all my needs. Even when my savings account seems to be washing away like dirt in a summer storm, I know you are in control. Whether it's cash or an item I need around the house, everything you give is a generous gift. I receive it and thank you for all you do. You are amazing! My circumstances may change, but you, Lord, never change. Steady and certain, you are totally reliable. Thank you. I praise you. In Jesus's name. Amen.

GENEROUS GIVING

Remember this: Whoever sows sparingly will also reap sparingly, and whoever sows generously will also reap generously.

2 Corinthians 9:6

Lord, I want to be a generous giver. Please help me to give generously in my tithe and gifts so that the resources you provide will get to the hands of those in need—those in missions, those in poverty, friends and family members who need help, and others I do not know or may never meet but who receive help through the charities and organizations to which I give. Help me to sow generously and reap generously. Help me to sow seeds of great love so I can also reap love. I ask in Jesus's name. Amen.

GET OUT OF DEBT

The rich rule over the poor,
    and the borrower is slave to the lender.

Proverbs 22:7

Lord, I need help getting out of debt. The bills are piling up. I feel like I am in quicksand and I keep sinking deeper. Sometimes I feel so embarrassed, like I should be able to provide for myself. I am realizing that being in debt is like being in bondage to the person or company to whom I owe money. I want to be free! I know that nothing is too hard for you; you are God Almighty. So I ask for wisdom and self-control, to get out of debt and to get ahead. I am trusting you and totally relying on you. Please help me. I ask in Jesus's mighty and powerful name. Amen.

STOP ARGUING ABOUT MONEY

Let us therefore make every effort to do what leads to
peace and to mutual edification.

Romans 14:19

*Lord, I am tired of arguing with my spouse over money. We are so
different! Savers and spenders disagree on how finances should work.
Please help us to communicate clearly and adjust our expectations.
Give us each respect for the other person despite our differences.
We are a team, a partnership, and I want to get back to that—and
learn to trust each other again. Please give us a better attitude about
money and the willingness to compromise and be flexible. I ask in
Jesus's name. Amen.*

BLESS MY FINANCES

Honor the LORD with your wealth,
> with the firstfruits of all your crops;
then your barns will be filled to overflowing,
> and your vats will brim over with new wine.

Proverbs 3:9–10

*Lord, I ask and pray in the name of Jesus that you would bless my
finances. Show me how to honor you with my money. Teach me
to manage my resources rightly so I save, spend, and give wisely.
You own it all; show me how to be a steward of what is yours for
good purposes. I choose to believe that your promises are true
for me, not just for everyone else, and that you will provide for
me. Thank you for your provision and wisdom. In Jesus's name.
Amen.*

TITHING AND GIVING

Honor God with everything you own;
> give him the first and the best.

Proverbs 3:9 Message

Lord, everything comes from your generous hand, even my ability to have income. So I choose to honor you in my tithing to the church and my giving to other ministries or organizations in need. I give you the firstfruits of my labor, right off the top. I give you my best, out of obedience to your Word and out of my heart's desire to give and serve with joy. I ask for abundance and increase so I can be an increasingly generous giver for your glory. In Jesus's name. Amen.

HOPE IN GOD

Command those who are rich in this present world not to be arrogant nor to put their hope in wealth, which is so uncertain, but to put their hope in God, who richly provides us with everything for our enjoyment.

1 Timothy 6:17

Lord, please forgive me for any pride or conceit I have about my finances. Whether I have money or not, help me to put my hope in you, not in riches or possessions. Those things can bring uncertainty; you, Lord, are strong and steadfast. I may not always be rich in money, but I am truly rich in my relationship with you—and all the good things you provide for me. Despite challenging circumstances, you are my peace. And I thank you. In Jesus's name. Amen.

THANK YOU, LORD!

Then call on me when you are in trouble,
    and I will rescue you,
    and you will give me glory.

Psalm 50:15 NLT

Lord, I am so grateful that you are totally trustworthy. When my life is a mess, when my finances are out of balance, or when the stock market is plunging and rising like a roller coaster, you are always with me. When I am in a jam, you save me and help me through. Even in my greatest desperation, you come through, and I give you all the glory. Thank you, Lord. In Jesus's name. Amen.

21

When Things Go Right

Prayers for Keeping the Faith in Victory and Success

As for me, I will always have hope;
I will praise you more and more.

Psalm 71:14

Throughout this book, you've sought the Lord and prayed when things have been dire and desperate. You may still be going through tough times, but as your life improves—relationships seem more stable, you finally get a new job, or you feel healthier—will you still rely on God? When things go right, will you stay close to God?

It can happen unexpectedly. You don't mean to ignore God, but you get busy with other things, and soon that special, precious relationship with God that you clung to like a lifeline in life's storms is but a distant memory during the sunshine of brighter days. Without forming words, you are saying, "I'm okay now, Lord. Thanks for the help. I can handle it from here."

That sort of pride and self-reliance, even in small doses, hurts the heart of our Savior.

Imagine doing the same thing to a close friend. You want her to be there for you when you're pouring out your problems and in need of help. But when you're fine, you drop her friendship like a hot potato. No friend wants that; neither does the Lord.

Staying close to God in the good times, not just the hard times, happens as we remember the importance of gratitude, giving, and staying connected to God in prayer.

Gratitude. When things start to go right, when God answers prayer, thank him for all he has done for you. An attitude of gratitude is essential. Regardless of your fluctuating emotions or the unpredictable economy, you can be thankful. Make a list of what God has done for you, and joy and gratitude will start bubbling up. Or read the book of Psalms. It is brimming with verses about real people who went through hard times and then spoke—or sang—their praise and gratitude to God. What are you thankful for today? Are you appreciative of all that God has done in your life—and is doing?

Giving. A grateful heart is moved to help others in need. Other-centered living reaches beyond natural tendencies of self-centeredness and reveals itself through a gift of time, a listening ear, or financial resources. When things start going better for you, don't forget about others who are still in need. Giving doesn't have to involve a lot of money or a huge gesture. Even a small amount can seem like a lot to someone who has little. The interesting thing about giving is that our words and actions have a ripple effect. The results are far-reaching—often more than we will ever know.

Staying connected to God in prayer. In nature, and in life, seasons come and go. But no matter what season of life you're in—the tough times or the good times—you can choose to stay connected to God in prayer and have hope.

When I was growing up in Wisconsin, I'd often ride my bike past our neighborhood's apple orchard. In every season, I'd watch the changes taking place, from the sweet-smelling apple blossoms in springtime to the crisp days in autumn that brought juicy, ripe apples. All year long, we'd wait with expectancy for the fruit to come. Growing took time, but it was always worth the wait.

As you release your cares to God, talking with him about your worries and fears, you are planting seeds of faith in the soil of hope—faith that one day your seed prayers will grow and come to fruition. That's the nature of hope, believing God will provide, that he will answer *above and beyond* what you've asked for. You may get one fruit-bearing tree or an entire apple orchard—bushel baskets of answered prayers! "For the LORD your God will bless you in all your harvest and in all the work of your hands, and your joy will be complete" (Deut. 16:15).

And so we pray. And as we wait on God, we mature. We grow up on the inside. Character is formed and trust grows. Just as we anticipate the day when round, red fruit will ripen, we look forward with hope to the moment our answers will be ready for picking. You and I may be praying about the same thing, but our answers may look different—just like apple trees bear different kinds of apples, like Braeburn, McIntosh, or Red Delicious.

We wait with hope, expectant that good things will happen, that one day things will be different, better. This side of heaven we live with the mystery of God's ways. Why does he do what he does? Why didn't he prevent that tragedy? *Why, Lord, why?* While we can know Christ, we cannot always be privy to his thoughts. And we can learn to trust him, even when we do not understand.

Our wild hope is that one day we will burst forth from time into eternity and be with the Lord, joyful and sorrow-free for all eternity. Despite hard things, and in the midst of tough times, believe that God has more for you than you can imagine. His power is at work within you, and the glory—the praise and the credit—goes to God for all he has done.

Wild hope means planting seeds of faith and expecting orchards of blessings. It's courageous and expectant—and celebratory—knowing that your great expectations aren't too large for the great big God we serve. Jesus Christ is our true Wild Hope. Unpredictable? Yes. Unexpected. Certainly. He goes beyond—far beyond—all we can imagine and leads us into a future we never could have dreamed of.

In times of defeat, doubt, or discouragement, pray. In times of joy and victory, pray. Know that your prayers really do make a difference. Trust the God of abundance, the God of so much more.

Harvest time is coming.

Dormant Dreams

Desires and dreams encased in a seed,
Released in the black earth of faith.
Time to let go of what I think I need,
And hold on to the hope of his grace.

Longingly gazing at empty brown dirt
Can't make your dreams grow any faster.
For the seed in the soil is dormant, not dead.
Look up, to the face of the Master.

Call out for courage, have patience, have faith!
A mystery's unveiling, my friend.
For a small, simple seed can yield sunflower gold.
Surely, this isn't the end.

In the fullness of time, resurrection.
The earth births a tender young shoot.
Nurtured and tended with strong, loving hands,
The flower grows deep, solid roots.

And the seedling unfolds to a blossom,
Pure artistry formed in the dark.
In his perfect timing the Harvester brings
Fruition to desires of the heart.

Jackie M. Johnson

OVERFLOWING WITH HOPE

May the God of hope fill you with all joy and peace as you trust in him, so that you may overflow with hope by the power of the Holy Spirit.

Romans 15:13

Lord, I want to overflow with hope! No matter what I am going through or how hard life gets, I can put my trust in you. And you fill me with joy and peace. What a blessing. Thank you! You are gener-ous, not stingy or sparse. You provide. I pray for the power of the Holy Spirit to help me overcome and find triumph and victory. I ask in Jesus's name. Amen.

GOD OF ABUNDANCE

And God is able to bless you abundantly, so that in all things at all times, having all that you need, you will abound in every good work.

2 Corinthians 9:8

Lord, thank you that you are my Wild Hope. You have all power and authority, and I ask for abundance and blessing in my life. I ask for favor in my health and finances, in my work and relationships. Bless me, Lord, with your goodness so I can do your will and be a blessing to others. In Jesus's name. Amen.

A HARVEST OF BLESSINGS

For the LORD your God will bless you in all your harvest and in all the work of your hands, and your joy will be complete.

Deuteronomy 16:15

Lord, you are good, the Lord of the harvest. I ask that you would bless me in the work of my hands; may all I do and say bring you glory and accomplish your purposes. Lord, I love you. I thank you for all you are doing in my life and all that is to come. You bring me joy. In Jesus's name. Amen.

NEVER GIVE UP

Let us not become weary in doing good, for at the proper time we will reap a harvest if we do not give up.

Galatians 6:9

Lord, I have been through so much, and you have given me the strength never to give up. Your power in me helps me to persevere and press on. You give me energy when I am tired, hope when I feel defeated. I have planted seeds of faith, Lord. Turn them into a harvest of blessings. Help me not to miss all that you have for me in this life. Let me gather in your goodness. I praise you! Thank you. In Jesus's name. Amen.

MORE TO COME

"What no eye has seen, what no ear has heard, and what no human mind has conceived"—the things God has prepared for those who love him.

1 Corinthians 2:9

Lord, thank you that you are a God of good surprises. I cannot imagine what you have in store for me in the future—both here on earth and in heaven forever with you. You have prepared things in advance for me because you love me. Thank you. I put my trust in you and totally rely on you. Lead me, Lord. Let us walk this life together with joy. In Jesus's name. Amen.

PRAISE GOD!

Now to him who is able to do immeasurably more than all we ask or imagine, according to his power that is at work within us, to him be glory in the church and in Christ Jesus throughout all generations, for ever and ever! Amen.

Ephesians 3:20–21

Lord, I don't even know where to begin to thank you. I think of all the times you've gotten me out of a jam, healed a broken relationship, or provided in unexpected ways. You are amazing! And even more so, you tell me that your power is at work within me. That is hard to comprehend, and yet I am so grateful. May your wonder-working power bring light to my life for all to see, that people may see—and experience—the goodness of God. For your glory. In Jesus's name. Amen.

THANK YOU, LORD

Give thanks to the LORD for his unfailing love
and his wonderful deeds for mankind,
for he satisfies the thirsty
and fills the hungry with good things.

Psalm 107:8–9

Lord, how can I begin to thank you for all you have done for me? Your love never fails; it stays with me always. Your acts on my behalf astound me as you provide when I am in great need. When I thirst for you, you fill me up with contentment and joy. When I am hungry, you satisfy me with the best gift ever—your close presence. I love you. Thank you for all you do and all you are. In Jesus's name. Amen.

OUR FAITHFUL GOD

For this God is our God for ever and ever;
he will be our guide even to the end.

Psalm 48:14

Lord, you are my faithful God. You are loving, accepting, kind, and compassionate. You are holy and just. You know all things. The galaxies were created as the work of your hands. You color the sky with rainbows. Your power is demonstrated in the rolling thunder and the jagged flashes of lightning. You lead and you provide. You heal and you connect. Thank you for being my guide even to the end. I give you all my praises. In Jesus's name. Amen.

Notes

Chapter 2 When You're Busy and Stressed

1. Mark Buchanan, *The Rest of God* (Nashville: Thomas Nelson, 2006), 93.

Chapter 3 When Life Is a Mess

1. Michael Yaconelli, *Messy Spirituality* (Grand Rapids: Zondervan, 2007), 69.

Chapter 5 When You're Depressed

1. Kristen Jane Anderson, with Tricia Goyer, *Life, in Spite of Me* (Colorado Springs: Multnomah, 2010), 165.
2. Ibid. If you are experiencing major depression, you may need to contact a mental health professional in your area.
3. Centers for Disease Control and Prevention, www.cdc.gov/nchs/data/data briefs/db07.htm.
4. Centers for Disease Control and Prevention, www.cdc.gov/nchs/data/data briefs/db07.htm#Definitions.
5. Beth Moore, *Believing God* (Nashville: LifeWay, 2002), 7.

Chapter 6 When You Feel Insecure

1. Jackie M. Johnson, *When Love Ends and the Ice Cream Carton Is Empty* (Chicago: Moody, 2010), 162.

Chapter 9 When You Feel Lonely

1. Gary R. Collins, *Christian Counseling: A Comprehensive Guide*, rev. ed. (Dallas: Word, 1988), 93.

Chapter 11 When You've Made Mistakes

1. Steven Furtick, *Sun Stand Still* (Colorado Springs: Multnomah, 2010), 153.
2. Jerry Bergman, Institute for Creation Research, "The Earth: Unique in All the Universe," www.icr.org/article/earth-unique-all-universe.

Chapter 13 When You Can't Break a Bad Habit or Addiction

1. http://en.wikipedia.org/wiki/Addiction#cite_note-5.
2. MedTerms Medical Dictionary, www.medterms.com/script/main/art.asp ?articlekey=101771.
3. Neil T. Anderson, *The Bondage Breaker* (Eugene, OR: Harvest House, 1993), 127–28.

Chapter 17 When You Have Health Concerns

1. Kim Painter, "Plant Seeds of Healing: Nature Makes You Feel Better," *USA Today*, April 15, 2007, www.usatoday.com/news/health/painter/2007-04-15-seeds -of-healing_N.htm.
2. Ibid.

Chapter 18 When You Have Job/Career Issues

1. George A. Buttrick, *Prayer* (Nashville: Abingdon Press, 1942).

Jackie M. Johnson is an author, blogger, and freelance writer in Colorado who brings hope and encouragement to readers worldwide. Her books include the popular *Power Prayers for Women*, *Powerful Prayers for Challenging Times*, and *When Love Ends and the Ice Cream Carton Is Empty*, a helpful breakup recovery resource. Connect with Jackie through her blog *Living Single* (www.drjamesdobson.org/blogs/living-single-blog) or website (www.jackiejohnsoncreative.com).